MW00973873

THE ENDING

THE TRUE STORY OF THE LIFE AND MURDER OF TOMMY MULLINS

For The Williams Family

By
JOAN C. MULLINS

Joan C Mullins

12 - 1 3 - 14

MURR PRINTING BEAUFORT PUBLISHING

Copyright © 2014 by Joan C. Mullins

All Rights Reserved. No part of this book
may be reproduced or transmitted in
any form or by and means electronic or
mechanical, including by photocopying, by
recording, or by any information storage
and retrieval system, without prior written
permission of the author and publisher,
except as permitted by United States of
America copyright law.

Published in the United States of America

ISBN-10: 0988249766

ISBN-13: 978-0-9882497-6-9

Book designed and manufactured by
MURR PRINTING BEAUFORT PUBLISHING

DEDICATION

This book is dedicated with love to Tommy,
my wonderful son, whose life was taken
so suddenly by a senseless murder.

TABLE OF CONTENTS

ACKNOWLEDGMENTS

I would like to say a heartfelt thank-you to my family
and friends for their encouragement and support.

To my editor, Tim Johnston, who believed in my story,
and with his caring help my book has become a reality.

MY TIME

As I lay there looking down at myself,
I begin to see the light. It draws closer and closer and
                    Then!!!
Almost without a sound, the light speaks.
I hear the low tone voice, but not with my ears...
I just hear it.
                    Strange...

Then I see my loved ones, but wait!!!
I have not seen them for years...at least,
That is, I cannot remember...
                    Strange...

It's almost like I'm floating. Suspended in space, I
I drift and drift. I feel at such speed...Why?
                    Strange...

My mind I can think so crystal clear,
No error...
No twice thinking,
I speak without talking,
Hear without listening,
See, without looking...

God, is it really my time?

                    Thomas L. Mullins, Jr.

INTRODUCTION

T.D. Johnston

On November 19th, 2010, Tommy Mullins of Bluffton, South Carolina, the fifty-year-old son of Joan C. Mullins, was murdered. Unarmed and disabled by back surgery and myriad maladies, he was shot in the chest from a distance of thirteen feet by a man twenty years his junior, who claimed to somehow be in imminent danger of death or serious injury at the hands of his disabled neighbor thirteen long feet away.

At some point in recent decades, American culture lost its common sense. Among many evidences of the backslide of our society, it became legal in a number of states to kill a human being, even an unarmed and disabled human being, under what is known as the Castle Doctrine. The idea that ending another person's existence is justified by the mere presence of that person on one's property is absurd, and yet absurdity becomes a legal accessory to murder when the absurd becomes law and common sense becomes a dead man's only defense.

Tommy Mullins was murdered for wanting his garage-door opener back. The justice system failed Tommy Mullins by not bringing his confessed killer to trial, and the killer is free to do it again any time someone comes to his door (as long as he tells the police that he felt "threatened," even by an unarmed man with multiple disabilities). Sadly, even when the Castle Doctrine is not applied, the simple presence of a spouse or significant other can provide a "witness" who justifies intentional homicide by siding with the killer. In this book by Tommy's mother, the reader will see a horrifying chain of events which leads to the death of an innocent man, and the unjust continued freedom of the man who murdered him.

Joan C. Mullins is a loving and devoted mother who has not been able to escape the double nightmare of tragic loss and gross injustice for nearly four years. The acceptance of the self-defense argument, without a trial, to excuse cold-blooded murder not only robs the innocent lives of those who are killed for no reason, but also forever harms the remaining days of those who care about those victims.

The loss of her son has devastated Joan C. Mullins. Further devastation has been wrought by the failure of the justice system to bring the killer, a confessed killer, to trial as prescribed by the Constitution. In writing this book, Joan C. Mullins seeks not only to honor her son's memory, but to help bring to light the tragic flaws in a justice system which allows one man to kill another and then claim self-defense, without evidence of a threat of serious bodily harm from the victim.

In this book the reader will also discover that a talented poet, devoted son, loving father and compassionate human being was cut short on that fateful evening in 2010.

I would like to have known Tommy Mullins, and am certain that I would have called him Friend.

PREFACE

My son, Thomas L. Mullins, was born on July 11, 1960 in Jersey City, New Jersey. He joined two sisters, Donna and Patricia, and a brother, Leonard.

When Tommy was three years old, the family moved to a lovely suburban home located in Hasbrouck Heights, New Jersey. It was so nice that we could move away from the city life.

So small was the town that all the schools were within walking distance.

Tommy was the average kid, like so many others. He was so excited to start school, so when his first day of kindergarten came about we walked those few blocks to the school; this was my little boy on a new adventure. I took him to his classroom and said goodbye, and told him I would be back to pick him up when school was done for the day.

This was so emotional. The time dragged on for me, as the house was silent and I could not wait until it was time to go pick him up. When the time came, up the hill I walked, making sure I was there ahead of time just to see him walk out of his class.

Well, I left a little boy that morning, and what emerged from his first day at school was a big kid saying "You know, Mom, you don't need to take me to and from school anymore. I can do this all by myself."

Of course he could. He was Tommy.

He joined the Cub Scouts, and I became the Den Mom. Lots of fun and laughter from that journey. He played the trombone. He taught himself how to play drums (his most favorite). He played football and baseball and joined all the happenings of school. He grew up to become a fine and good person and man. He liked to write poetry, and one of his poems received an Honorable Mention in an anthology out of California. The poem is called "My Time." He was so proud, and with good reason.

I would like to tell you how this book became about.

Tommy's health and life became problematic over the years. His dad and I moved to South Carolina when the company he worked for decided to change locations. We moved, leaving our four adult children behind, and this move was so hard for us all.

Tommy had married and divorced. He was a father of two sons, Michael and Thomas, and a daughter, Kaitlyn.

When Tommy's dad retired, his boredom led him to opening his own company. In time, Tommy and his brother moved to South Carolina to work for his dad. One day, Tommy had a stroke while at work. This started the chain of events for his body breaking down, and he no longer could work.

Eventually Tommy had to go on disability. He disliked having to do this...In this time frame his dad became ill with cancer, so my husband and I decided to move to Sun City in Bluffton, South Carolina, hoping life would be somewhat less stressful and that the continued chemotherapy would give him more time.

Three and a half years later, Tommy's dad died.

Tommy was still living in the area where his dad's shop was, and Tommy's life was going downhill. I asked Tommy if he would like to move to the town of Bluffton. When he said "Yes" I was so happy that he would be living near me. So when this new townhome was finished being built, he was glad to make the move. He was so happy with his life, finally feeling a little more secure.

Sadly, the events that took place at this home ended in devastation.

DISCLAIMER AND OTHER INFORMATION

This book is a work of non-fiction.

Only two names have been changed. All other names have been withheld entirely. Any resemblance to actual people living or dead is entirely coincidental.

In this book, the reader will find out all the facts that led up to Tommy's murder, in addition to:

Tommy's words said to me and his family members.

Places and incidents are all truth and facts with police reports, police tapes, texts, e-mails, court documents and newspaper accounts.

I received permission to use articles from newspapers.

Newspapers carried this whole story. Real names, naturally, appear in the newspaper accounts.

One of the prosecutors was totally unprofessional to me. I made a charge to the state about it, as detailed in this book. Sadly, the state said it was considered unfounded. Is it not a shame that a professional person can act in the way he did and get away with it? The justice system did not believe me. I tell the story in this book, referring to him as the second prosecutor. Because of this incident I asked for a new prosecutor. Now if the solicitor's office did not believe what had happened to me, they would not have had a new prosecutor take over, and when the solicitor's office said the change was made due to a conflict of interest, what else could they say?

I have e-mails from the third prosecutor's office refusing to send me a written statement confirming what was told to me. They felt that a phone call was sufficient and it was not. I did receive the law I asked for that he based one of the reasons upon, but why would he not pursue the case when the law the third prosecutor quoted does not apply to my son's case? They decided not to go forth with a trial, giving me a weak reason based on a legal case which was not similar to my son's.

When I asked for the immunity information (the killer's girlfriend was the only witness, and the third prosecutor had intended to offer her immunity in exchange for her testimony against the killer), they did not send the information, and now, on the verge of this book's publication, they still have refused to send it.

I am a victim, and have the right to be given information about the crime. I knew nothing about the police tape while the case was pending, and it was not until three years later that I found out about this audio evidence (this was the basis for the possible plea offer of immunity), and I was never informed of this. What can you say about our justice system?

This police tape recording has proven the innocence of my son and that two people had wanted him JUST DEAD.

AUTHOR'S NOTE

I am just a mom. For all of you parents out there, I am sure that you can either imagine or, sadly, in some cases even identify with, the agony of outliving a child. Writing this book has been an experience which is both painful and necessary. I owe it to my son, to myself, my family and our society to share this story.

I have decided not to use the real name of the person who killed my son. I have also decided not to use the real name of the person who was the killer's girlfriend, who played a significant role in bringing about the circumstances that resulted in the murder. Hence, the name I will use for the killer is "Wayne." The name I will use for the killer's girlfriend is "Lilith."

STREET PERSON

After Tommy lost his work in the family business, he tried to open his own construction company. A friend of his was interested, so they went forth with this dream.

They acquired what material they would need and found a first client, whose job was to complete a sidewalk.

This was not an easy job, as time showed they really did not have all the particular tools needed to keep a construction company floating. Nevertheless, it was finished and the client was happy with the job. But more jobs were just not out there. They also needed more materials, and with the lack of funds to keep this going, they had to give this idea up.

Tommy did not have a home, as he had to leave the apartment where he was living at that time, because he just could not afford a place living on the disability amount he received.

A friend had Tommy move in with him and his family, so with what little belongings Tommy owned, he had to put them in the garage. In time everything molded, and was completely ruined.

Of course this was not a good idea for either of them, so Tommy had to move. With no place to go he became a street person, living under the highway bridges and wherever he could find. At this time he also had his beloved dog Rocky, and life of course was terrible. I knew nothing of this, as he never complained.

Tommy had a nephew. His name was also Tommy, and my son was the godfather to him.

Somehow Tommy's nephew heard he was living on the street. He found Uncle Tom and brought him back to his home. Tommy stayed with him for about ten days, but the nephew had to ask him to leave, as money was getting tight with him also. So nephew Tom contacted Tommy's brother. He told him what was happening. Well, his brother of course had to do the right thing, and that was to get him into an apartment he could afford.

Moving into this complex, he acquired hand-me-downs and discarded furnishings from around the area. I really do not know how Tommy carried on with his life, as he never ever complained to me. My heart was broken to know he had gotten to this place in his life. And his health was really going down.

I decided that enough was enough for him, and asked Tommy if he wanted to move to the area I lived in. With his acceptance, I looked around. I was able to buy a new town house. I furnished it all for him, and this was to be his forever home. It was all to be his, as I was in the process of turning all paperwork over to him when he was killed.

Before you read of the events which led to my son's death, it is important for you to understand the law in South Carolina regarding when a person can use deadly force lawfully. These next two chapters reveal South Carolina law for defense of home, person and property.

PROTECTION OF PERSONS AND PROPERTY ACT
(South Carolina, enacted in 2006)

The stated intent of the legislation is to codify the common law castle doctrine, which recognizes that a person's home is his castle, and to extend the doctrine to include an occupied vehicle and the person's place of business. This bill authorizes the lawful use of deadly force under certain circumstances against an intruder or attacker in a person's dwelling, residence, or occupied vehicle. The bill provides that there is no duty to retreat if (1) the person is in a place where he has a right to be, including the person's place of business, (2) the person is not engaged in an unlawful activity, and (3) **the use of deadly force is necessary to prevent death, great bodily injury, or the commission of a violent crime.** A person who lawfully uses deadly force is immune from criminal prosecution and civil action, unless the person against whom deadly force was used is a law enforcement officer acting in the performance of his official duties and he identifies himself in accordance with applicable law or the person using deadly force knows or reasonably should have known the person is a law enforcement officer.

H.4301 (R412) was signed by the Governor on June 9, 2006.

WHAT IS THE CASTLE DOCTRINE?

(From an article by Paul Bowers in the Charleston City Paper)

In South Carolina, your home is your castle. So is your car, and so is your business. Under the state's interpretation of the "castle doctrine," as amended in 2006, civilians are allowed to use deadly force to defend themselves, but they have to meet certain requirements. Basically, if you are out in a neighborhood (like George Zimmerman, the neighborhood watch captain who shot and killed 17-year-old Trayvon Martin in Sanford, Fla., in February) or in another public place, you are on shaky legal ground if you pull out a weapon. And you are probably not getting off the hook if the incident happens in a place where you have no right to be.

But unlike some other states, in South Carolina you are not required to retreat before you come out with guns blazing at in your home, car, or business. That's why, as in Florida and 23 other states, this type of law is known as a "Stand Your Ground" law. Our state holds that a person who is being attacked in his castle "has no duty to retreat and has the right to stand his ground and meet force with force."

So, as the Clash would say, know your rights. Police can't arrest you for defending yourself unless they have probable cause to believe you were acting outside of the law. Here's when it's OK for a law-abiding citizen to open fire on an assailant:

WHERE: The law protects you from prosecution if you can **prove you were defending yourself** in one of the following places — provided you are an owner, resident, or invited guest:
- house
- apartment
- condo

- hotel room
- porch
- mobile home
- tent
- place of business
- vehicle, motorized or non-motorized

DANGER: A second **requirement** is that **your assailant must be putting you in danger of "great bodily injury," which the law defines as something that "creates a substantial risk of death or which causes serious, permanent disfigurement, or protracted loss or impairment of the function of a bodily member or organ."** You're clear to defend yourself with deadly force if your attacker is:

- in the process of unlawfully breaking and entering your home, vehicle, or business, or
- attempting to forcibly remove somebody from your home, vehicle, or business

WHO: You can't shoot somebody who is a lawful resident, owner, lessee, or titleholder of the place you are trying to defend. The law also doesn't protect you if you shoot someone for trying to remove his or her child, grandchild, or other person who is under his or her lawful custody or guardianship. And you can't shoot at an on-duty police officer.

A NEW HOME

My son, Tommy Mullins, finally was in his new home in Bluffton, accompanied by his dog, Rocky, a boxer all of a hundred pounds. What a beautiful animal he was, so large and strong. One time I tried to walk him in my back yard, and he pulled me over the berm.

Tommy was so happy to have a new home to call his. He had many disabilities and had not been able to work at all. So this home was a home he could finally feel happy in and be comfortable, especially having the extra bedroom for his daughter Katie for visits, with hopes that she would be able to attend the University of South Carolina at Beaufort. This way she could live with him.

Tommy also wanted to get back into writing poetry. He had received an honorable mention in an anthology out of California for his poem "My Time." He also loved and played drums; having a new home all his own would allow him to pursue this passion.

Tommy had been a member of a Baptist church in Spartanburg. He loved being part of this church, where he found Jesus and learned so much about the Bible that he and I had lots of conversations, especially about Revelations. Sometimes in our lives we do get lost from God and the Lord Jesus, but he is never far away and one day he is back in our lives. Such was the case for Tommy when he moved into his new home to begin his new life, near me, hopefully welcoming his daughter, and always with his companion, Rocky. And he had found a church that was just right for him. I joined him every Sunday, singing hymns that brought tears to each of us, and he would yell out "Amen!" as many others had when the pastor was giving his sermon.

The church was looking for a drummer to take over the position that needed to be filled. Tommy tried out, and was thrilled when he was accepted to be part of this band; he said he felt a little nervous and could not wait until Sunday came to begin.

He was to become a member of this Baptist church in Bluffton, and was to play with the band that very next Sunday. He was to play five songs on this day, including his favorite, "Amazing Grace," but when Sunday arrived he was having colon problems, so he was not able to play. But he became a member of the Church this day, and was able to do this, and felt so good about being a part of his new church. He was scheduled to play the upcoming Sunday as a new member of the band and as a new member of the church family. Life was on the upswing for my son, despite all of the afflictions and disabilities he had borne throughout his adult life. But the next Sunday never came for Tommy. It never came because five days later he was murdered.

Let me tell you what it was like to be my son prior to being killed for wanting his garage-door opener back. This may also provide an indication of his inability to be a real threat to the killer, who took his life anyway.

Some growths had been found during a colonoscopy. The growths were removed and thank goodness they were non-cancerous, but sadly he had also developed Barrette's Disease, a condition of the esophagus that eventually would turn into cancer. He also had very bad sleep apnea. He suffered a stroke while working in his dad's machine shop. He was working on the lathe machine when he collapsed, and was unable to function well enough to ever work again.

Weeks before he was killed, Tommy had a terrible attack of colitis. The bleeding was so bad that he almost died. Eventually the doctor found the area that caused this attack when he had his colon exam, and by that time it was healing slowly.

Imagine being told, after a debilitating stroke, contending every night with sleep apnea, and a colitis attack on top of that, that your bowel has fallen and now is hanging out of your body. How would you feel? Can you imagine how Tommy felt? Unfortunately, Tommy's afflictions didn't stop there.

Tommy also needed to have replacements of both of his hips, and had several cysts in one shoulder. To compound his physical suffering, he had a very bad back due to a fall down the stairs several years earlier, narrowly missing the area where he would have been paralyzed to never walk again, but damaging the spine in ways which made movement and walking difficult, especially with the debilitated hips and the ongoing challenges from his stroke.

Over the years, Tommy was in constant pain, but finally found a doctor who treated Tommy with pain injections every three months to help control the pain. The pain could not, however, be fully alleviated because Tommy had allergies to several of the more effective pills.

Being in pain every day, Tommy simply decided that life goes on whether you are feeling well or not, so every day he managed to get through all this. He had his happiness just in getting out and taking Rocky for his walks, and practicing his drums for his debut as a member of the church band. He would drive over to see me almost every day, which made me very happy. And once a month, he presented me with beautiful bouquets of flowers. He was such a wonderful son.

I have two Yorkies, Mira and Winston. They loved to play with Rocky. He loved them; he was so gentle and seemed to know that they were so tiny. When they would play with each other, Rocky would take Mira's head in his mouth. This was always funny; he was ever so good with them, much like Tommy was always so kind and gentle with animals and people alike.

Tommy loved to cook and he would make great meals and he would call me up and say "Mom, I made spare ribs, so come on over and eat with me." He would make his potato salad, served with a green salad, and it was always fabulous. He also would share his cooking with the neighbors.

Every now and then we enjoyed having a little contest: which one of us could make the best tastiest meatballs or potato salad? How wonderful it was that I could live so close to him. Yes, his meatballs were really tasty and he always liked my potato salad, so finally he was able to make it the same way.

We would go out once a month finding pizza restaurants, seeking to determine the best-tasting pizza around. It was becoming quite a tradition for Tommy and me.

The community to which Tommy moved was fast-growing with new homes. After Tommy moved in, three guys and one gal bought homes all next to each other. All became friends. One of the guys was a collector of rifles and guns, and he would go range shooting; Tommy became interested in this hobby, so he applied for a permit to purchase a gun; he had to go to Hilton Head Island to attend an all-day class. He passed the test, so he now was able to purchase a gun and join his friend for shooting at the range.

He would complain that his back would hurt badly after shooting, but he would say it's worth it just to be out and alive. My son was happy, even with the pain and the physical limitations he endured, to be "back in the game of life."

By this time, Tommy started having some serious issues with his back, finding out that he would need multiple surgeries, one of the more serious being to remove a large cyst that caused so much pain that he could hardly walk. So on his fiftieth birthday I drove him to Charleston for his surgery. The year before I gave him a 49/50th (strange I did this but felt he would think something was up for his 50th) surprise birthday and his lifetime buddies from New Jersey made the trip down to South Carolina. They filmed it and called it "Trip to the Moon." As a kid in school Tommy was called Moon Mullins. Ironically, he was now living on a street called Moon Beam Drive.

OH NO

Before my son became the tragic victim of homicide, he and I both fell victim in another way. This might give you an indication of his trusting personality, which connects with the tragedy which awaited him.

My son Tommy was settling into his new home, and finally had the Internet connected to the world; he could not wait to contact his buddies in New Jersey to give them his new address.

After a few weeks, he told me he started conversing to some gal he met through a singles group in Africa. This person said she had to walk miles to get to a free Internet service just to speak with him, as she lived in a poor area with no transportation. (I checked the town out that she claimed she lived in and there was one by that name)

Tommy forwarded her picture and she looked like a sweet person. But being a mother, I of course could not keep my thoughts to myself, therefore cautioning him.

"Oh Mom, I know," Tommy said.

As the months passed he would continue to send me these lovely letters she wrote to him, and many more pictures so I could see that it was a "real" conversation going on.

One day we decided to go out for lunch. My son sat quiet, not his usual self, and I asked what was wrong.

"Oh!" he said with tears. "I just would like to have love in my life again." He said that his gal offered to him that she would be willing to come to the U.S. to care for him, as my son had many health problems, but she needed to get a work visa and could only stay six months, or maybe marry. So she asked him if he could help her get a visa, but it involved sending her funds, so this lunch day turned into us going to get a moneygram of $1,500 for the visa and plane fare.

The next day the information came with the flight number and day she was to depart.

Another few days passed, then an email with a contract of some sort, saying that this needed to be signed and more funds were needed in case something might happen to her, ending up in a wrong state or whatever might happen to luggage lost and funds for a hotel stay if indeed there was a mixup. Cost was $3,000.

Before my son told me about the contract, I had already called the airlines about this reservation, as somehow I began thinking things just do not seem right. Of course they were not. There was not a plane reservation or anybody by that name or a visa.

I contacted this person myself to tell him what I had found out about not having the reservations, and then his explanation was that that was why he sent a contract.

This male person who was to be sponsoring her from Africa emailed me back to say everything was legitimate and that the other funds were needed before she could get on the plane, as this would be proof that we in faith would take care of her.

"Oh no," I said, realizing that we had been scammed. I told them they were scammers and that we had no intentions of sending any other funds to them, and that I would report them.

A day later this man begins telling us that the gal's mother was screaming and crying, as how could we do this to her daughter, not to give her a chance?

They were thinking we would give in to them by feeling sorry.

Of course this would not happen.

It is an awful sinking feeling to know how easy it is to be fooled, taken, even though I had suspected this did not seem right. I wanted to help my son.

Of course my son was more than upset, as I gave him the funds to help him do this.

They would not let up on us, and finally we blocked any mail from them.

I called the U.S. Consulate and left a message describing what happened to us, telling of this horrible story. They responded with a phone call back to me, asking to give them more facts. After listening, the woman said "Yes, this was a scam." I said I felt so bad for my son, as he was taken in as well as I. I knew how his trust was in this person, to think she was coming to help him, and he felt more than a fool. I told him not to be concerned anymore, because this guy got nothing more from us.

I was told to look further on the Internet under Scams, and to my horror, it was unbelievable the number of people that are scammed every day, and not just for little amounts of monies, but $50,000 and more.

So many of us are caring and trusting people, and we do not think that seemingly nice people are criminals until we are scammed.

AFTER HIS SURGERY

T ommy's surgery to remove the large cyst was successful. We were pleased to hear this, but the doctor told Tommy that he should not be going up and down the stairs with his back and hips in their condition. Then came some more bad news: he would eventually have to use a wheelchair.

Tommy had already put the house up for sale before the surgery, as he really wanted to move to a place that was all on one floor. Sadly, the only people coming to look were asking to rent, but the sale was what was needed in order to buy another home.

Tommy said, "Mom, don't worry about coming to walk Rocky." Unfortunately, when Tommy uttered those words, I had no idea that this was the beginning of the end for my son.

Lilith was the gal that moved there. She volunteered to walk Rocky during the time of Tommy's recovery, so she asked Tommy to give her his door opener to the garage. This way she could come and take Rocky for a walk as needed. Well, one day she let herself in and went up to Tommy's bedroom to get Rocky. Tommy, having sleep apnea, could not hear anything as the CPAP machine makes a noise when used. He was jolted awake by Rocky carrying on, and when he looked up he saw Lilith standing over his bed. Tommy said "Do not ever come up to my bedroom again. You can call Rocky from downstairs, as Rocky was in a defend move and this was not a situation to be in." Lilith taking the liberty to come into his bedroom was not the correct thing to do, either.

The dog-walking lasted a while, until finally Tommy said, "I do not need you to walk Rocky anymore." He took his door opener back, and thought that was the end of it. But Lilith carried on for a few weeks, saying "I want to do this, Tommy," so Tommy gave in, and once more she had the garage door opener in her possession. He really did not want to, as he told me on several occasions, but she cried and said she could not understand why he did not want her to do this anymore. All in all, Tommy just wanted to be friends with her, and to keep the peace.

As time passed, Lilith's boyfriend, who worked for the same company as Lilith, moved into her home. It was at this time that Lilith was entering Tommy's home any time she wanted, using the garage door opener whenever the house was locked. Tommy did not like this anymore, and in time he asked for the door opener back once again. She would not give it to him. This created a problem, which grew when Lilith discovered something she wanted in Tommy's house.

Tommy was prescribed Xanax for anxiety. Lilith knew this. She started asking Tommy to share his pills with her, saying that she would get her prescription from her doctor, and she promised that she would give the amount back that she borrowed from him. Alas, but she did not do it. To complicate matters, she told Tommy that she knew a UPS guy who wanted pills too, so this started to get very tricky, to say the least. It sounded like pills were possibly being sold.

Tommy by this time had bought a lock box in which to keep his medicines. He told Lilith that he would not give her any more pills.

The night before the murder, Lilith emailed a neighbor to see if he had any Xanax. By this time it appeared that she had become somewhat desperate. Her email to the neighbor, asking for Xanax when she no longer could get it from Tommy, is on file with the police.

The week before Tommy died, he came to visit me, as per his usual schedule. He just sat for the longest time in the chair, really looking upset, and then said he could not take this anymore and explained the story about the Xanax, and that Lilith was taking other drugs and Tommy was trying to talk her out of what she was doing.

Evidently things were not good, as he simply did not want her around, and told her to stay away from him and Rocky. She just would not leave Tommy alone; in the meantime, she was playing her boyfriend and Tommy against each other.

Wayne at times would come and bang on Tommy's door, yelling for Lilith, but she was never there on these occasions. But what is hard to realize is that about two weeks before the murder, Wayne and Lilith sat in Tommy's home eating pizza.

Three days before his murder, Tommy told me that Lilith wanted to meet with him at Wendy's to discuss or talk about what was going on. He went, and when Tommy talked to me that night, he told me things were escalating. Tragically, three days later I knew exactly what he meant.

I was talking with him at 5:15 on the day of his murder. He started to tell me more about the situation with Lilith, and then he said "Oh. Lilith." It sounded like she was calling in on his other line. Then he said, "Mom, I will call you later." Oh, what horrible things could have happened in the space of four hours.

I had not heard back from Tommy by eight in the evening, and I thought "I will call him." But then I thought, "Well, I will hear from him in the morning." Like clockwork, Tommy called me every morning by eight o'clock. I have felt guilt from not calling him, as I might have been able to save his life. Tommy was killed shortly after nine in the evening, so I will never know whether my calling him that night would have prevented the tragedy.

The police came to my home at around eleven o'clock that night. I was sleeping when the ringing of the doorbell woke me up. Going to the door, I saw two policemen standing there with badges showing. I opened the door and they asked my name.

"Yes," I said. "I am Joan Mullins."

"We are sorry that we have some bad news. Your son was in an accident."

"No!" I cried out. "Was he driving his car?"

"No," they said. "His neighbor shot him. He is dead."

Everything just became a blur. They suggested I not stay alone so I called my brother and a friend.

How can a person ever sleep after this terrible news? It was around 4:30 in the morning, and I was awake, crying, when the phone rang. It was the donor bank, asking if I would donate organs from Tommy. His body was so shot apart, so I said all I could donate would be his eyes. If anything, his eyes would be able to help some person and, if not, would go to research. A few weeks later, I received a donor medal that was created to honor the memory of those whose ultimate act of human kindness helped improve the lives of others through organ and tissue donation. This was a Gift Of Life, and I was told that lives have been dramatically improved by this generosity, which is a living memory of the loved one who has passed. Tommy had signed up to be a Gift Of Life donor when he received his driver's license.

Having to call family members, especially Tommy's sister Donna, was extremely difficult, as she and her husband were coming to visit on Saturday, and we were all going to a sports bar to watch the Giants game. The Giants were Tommy's favorite team, and he and his sister were so looking forward to seeing each other, so to tell them what happened and that Tommy was dead—how could I do this?

All I remember is saying, "Tommy was killed." Then, to hear the horror of Donna screaming and crying was more than I could bear, as we were not near each other, to hold each other during this horrid time.

Making arrangements for his funeral was something I don't even remember doing. This was a reality that I could not accept. I remember the funeral home calling and asking me to bring a shirt for Tommy to be laid out in. I somehow found myself at Wal-Mart, racks of shirts in front of me, searching for something special, one I knew he would like. Tommy's favorite colors were black and white. And then there it was, just so perfect. I knew Tommy would like this one.

On Sunday the funeral home filled with family and visitors. It was so hard just seeing Tommy laying there with this smile on his face, looking like he could just sit up and say "Hi!" in his friendly way at any second. I patted his arms and hands and kissed his forehead. This would be the last time I would be able to hug my baby, his human body, telling him that I loved him, looking at him as a person in addition to the beautiful soul he is and will always be.

The pastor gave his prayers, and in an instant all of this part was over with. Now he was to be cremated and laid to rest next to his dad at the columbarium. I asked that a poem which Tommy wrote, "My Time", be put in with his ashes as this was his own eulogy, which he wrote without ever thinking that it would be used in this way.

That night the killer was arrested; he himself called the police and said he shot his neighbor. Before the EMTs arrived, Tommy's next-door neighbor told me that his (the neighbor's) dogs began barking at the door, and when he opened it he saw Tommy on the ground. He ran to him and started CPR. Later he told me he knew Tommy was not going to make it, but that he felt he had to try to administer CPR anyway. The neighbor also said that Lilith stood over Tommy and said, "I am sorry, Tommy." My God. What did she mean by this remark? "I'm sorry I got you killed?" "I'm sorry Wayne needlessly took your life?" Or just "That's too bad you're dead, Tommy?" Or was it sarcastic? Was the guilt already there, or was she part of his killing, revealed by not calling the police herself? She had choices that evening, just like Wayne did. She knew that Wayne would get his gun to kill Tommy, and yet she did nothing to stop him from murdering my son.

I will always be sick in my heart, wondering what Tommy must have been thinking when Wayne pulled the gun on him. Did he think he would actually fire the gun? If so, did his life flash before his eyes? Did he think, "I'm unarmed. All I want from you is my garage-door opener?" One thing is for sure. My son was not given time to protest the idea of being gunned down in cold blood. He was not given time to walk thirteen more feet to ask Wayne to give him the gun and talk like civilized people.

Oh God, but I still think of the pain as he died, and the loneliness of dying away from his loved ones.

A few days after the murder, I was standing in the kitchen when I heard Tommy's voice say "Ma? Ma? What happened?" I turned around, believing I would actually see him there. I said, "Wayne murdered you."

While driving down the road one day, I started crying. Then I heard Tommy's voice say "Oh Ma, don't cry." Tommy would often say this to me when we were in church and singing the beautiful hymns together. It was hard not to cry on those occasions, and I find that it is always painful to cry now. Beauty and tragedy both bring tears; injustice just makes the tears more bitter.

As I said before, all Tommy wanted was his door opener back and to be left alone by Lilith, who was creating a great deal of tension with her repeated and uninvited trips into his house in search of Tommy's prescription drugs. On the day of the murder, Tommy had just told her on the phone (documented) to stay away from him, but evidently she just aggravated him more that evening by looking for him. Claiming that she wanted to give him back the opener, she expanded the visit into an argument over the drugs she was taking, and Tommy tried to make her realize that she needed to stop.

She could not find Tommy when she entered his home, and after she went upstairs looking for him and came back down, Tommy was there. It was then that she claimed to the police that he threatened her with a gun.

According to the "Castle Law," a person has the right to approach a person who is in his or her home without permission, including to threaten or even kill the intruder. Lilith absolutely had no business being in his home, as this day he had told her several times not to bother him or Rocky or to come into his home anymore. All she did by entering his home was to aggravate him, as he had wanted nothing more than to have his garage door opener back and to be left alone.

At the murder scene, the police asked Lilith why she did not call the police when Tommy knocked at her door in his quest to retrieve his garage door opener. She said she didn't call the police because "Wayne would take care of it." And he did. Wayne shot him. Was this the plan all along, to kill Tommy and then claim Castle Doctrine or "Stand Your Ground" by saying that he attacked them?

Lilith took the Fifth. So what does this tell you? The police report reveals that she confessed that she saw Wayne kill Tommy, and that Tommy was unarmed. Once this information was known and admitted, it should have opened both her and Wayne up to all questions related to motive, since the physical fact that Wayne shot and killed Tommy point blank from thirteen feet was already established.

Wayne had a choice that evening: to call the police and stay in his home, instead of sneaking out and ambushing an unarmed man. Unfortunately, Wayne did not choose that prudent and reasonable, common-sense approach. Wayne deliberately went out of his home to kill Tommy. If he had simply called the police to say that a neighbor was "bothering them" to get his garage-door opener back, this horrible senseless murder would never have come about. The decision to sneak out of his garage and ambush Tommy with his Glock gun and blow him apart was at best reckless and at worst cold-blooded, calculated murder.

Wayne supposedly told the police that Tommy lunged at him. However, Lilith says that Tommy "took one step." In Tommy's health condition, with his disabilities, and having had back surgery, "one step" is all he could have managed with any speed at all. He would not have been able to get to Wayne. Not even close. It is sad to know that the justice system considers the murder of an unarmed man from a distance of thirteen feet to in any way be "justifiable." Sadder still is the willingness of investigators or prosecutors to let a case drop without any indication or evidence that the murder was justifiable.

Here is the only factual evidence from the murder scene: my son was shot from a distance of thirteen feet (fact). Tommy was unarmed (fact). He was physically incapacitated by his condition (fact). His neighbors knew of his disabled condition (fact). These are facts. It is ludicrous to suggest that somehow Tommy could possibly have made it all the way to Wayne, and then somehow still have the strength and energy to subdue the younger, healthier, armed man. But ludicrous as it is, that was the feeble, nonsensical explanation by Wayne for his homicidal action, ending Tommy's life from thirteen feet with a hollow-tipped bullet meant to blow apart the inside of any man or animal.

The killer was in jail for twelve days. *Twelve.* And then I was notified that he would be getting out on bail. His girlfriend's parents were paying his bond. The judge ordered him to live in his girlfriend's parents' home. Mind you, their home was just a little more than one block from mine. Telling Wayne he was not to come within one thousands yards of me and then ordering him to live down the street was nonsensical and an insult to me.

I'll share a bit of unhelpful instruction from the judge here. The judge said, "Oh yes, Ms. Mullins, by all means, if you are to see him ride by your home, let us know." Can you imagine this? What a slap in the face to have the killer of my son living right down the block from me. I was going to be a witness in the trial, as I knew much that could help the prosecution put this killer away. To be forced to put up with him as a new neighbor was infuriating.

I wrote many letters asking that he be moved out of my area. Finally, *finally*, after over three months, they were answered and the killer was ordered to move back into his girlfriend's house.

WHAT MUST TOMMY HAVE THOUGHT IN HIS FINAL SECONDS?

W hat might Tommy have said or thought as he died for no good reason? Can you imagine what, for the few seconds he might have had, his mind was asking? I can imagine, sadly:

"Why? All I wanted was my garage door opener back..."

I lost my son over something that could have been talked about sensibly, as Tommy had tried many times to do, but Lilith just did not care. All she did was make matters worse. Tommy told her not to bother with him on the day he was killed, but she had to enter his home yet again, looking and trespassing, unable to find him. And then my son appeared during her trespassing, wondering what in the world she was doing in his home yet again. After the fact, she claimed that he threatened her with a gun. If such a claim were true, why would he leave the gun at home if he meant to harm Wayne minutes later when Tommy came to their house asking yet again for the return of his garage door opener?

The frustration of asking over and over again for the return of his property was not fun for Tommy. Finally, he left a message, minutes before his death, that if they didn't give him his door opener back immediately he would call the police. As he lay dying, he must have wished he had called the police, or that Wayne and Lilith had called the police if they felt in any way threatened by his coming over in search of his property. A terrible and senseless tragedy, followed by lies from the killers, would have been avoided.

But Tommy did what good neighbors do. He didn't call the police on them. He came over to ask yet again that they return his property. And then he was ambushed. He lost his life, and I lost my son.

"Why, God? Why would people shoot me just to avoid letting me call the police? Why, God? These killers will get to say goodbye to their mothers, while I must lay here and listen to them talk about what to say to the police to cover their motivation for killing me. Why must people be so selfish, so evil? Goodbye, Mom. I love you..."

I wrestle with what my son experienced at the end. The pain. The loss of breath and sight. The loneliness of dying without the presence of his loved ones. My son is in Heaven. I know that. But here on Earth I miss him.

We should not accept the actions of cowards. What a coward the killer is. He blew apart the chest of an innocent, unarmed, disabled man.

TOMMY'S HEALTH AT THE TIME OF HIS MURDER

A t the time of his death, Tommy was dealing with multiple health issues, as indicated previously in this book. Because they point to the reasons why he was no threat to the killer or his girlfriend unless he had a gun with him or had entered their home (neither being the case), I list them here:

Tommy suffered from: sleep apnea, Barrette's disease (pre-cancer), the need for replacement of both hips, cysts in his shoulder, diverticulitis, an extremely bad back, high blood pressure, eye damage caused by a stroke, and bowel distention.

Obviously he was in no condition to somehow overpower and cause serious bodily harm to a healthy 31-year-old man, nor was he inside the 31-year-old man's house to have any chance to inflict harm in the first place. According to the Castle Doctrine, such threat must be imminent to justify a shooting. Not only was it not imminent, or even possible, but the killer aggressively left his home and shot my unarmed son with a hollow-tipped bullet designed to blow apart the inside of a body.

It should also be noted here that fist marks were on Tommy's door, from the killer banging on it on previous occasions in the belief that his girlfriend was in Tommy's house. On none of those door-banging occasions did Tommy exit his home with a gun and shoot his neighbor. Food for thought.

A LETTER TO TOMMY'S PASTOR

I wrote the following letter to Tommy's pastor, in gratitude for the outpouring of sorrow and condolences from the congregation:

Dear Pastor Mark,

I wanted to thank you and to give my Love to the people that gave sorrows to me for Tommy's murder.

I wanted to let them know of Tommy's and my first visit to your church, and, Pastor Mark, when your message preaching of Jesus and healing that day, I cried and Tommy hugged me and said, "Mom, what is the matter?" I said, "I wish Jesus were here to heal you." I thought back to that morning and realized that he did heal both Tommy and me, not physically but in our hearts we both always believed, but it was very different that morning, so special to us.

Tommy felt comfort in this church, and he wanted to join as soon as possible. You and Tommy visited on Tuesdays. Tommy talked about the lessons to me that he was to complete. He wanted so much to be part of this church, and to be finding a home once again.

Every Sunday I went churching with Tommy. He would call me and say, "Mom, are you going with me tomorrow?" "Of course," I replied. I realized he needed me at this time, and each Sunday I would cry as we sang the hymns, and he would look at me with tears and eyes red. The Lord had touched us both.

He was a wonderful son who was ill and in pain. He was ill the day he became a member, and this day he was to play drums, but he felt too sick to do this. The next day he called the doctor and was prescribed medication, and by Wednesday he started to feel good again, and was so looking forward to playing drums that Sunday.

Tommy emailed me the music that was to be presented on Sunday. I felt confident he would play well. I told him that "Amazing Grace" was one song I loved. Friday he was murdered. The short time he had with the church I know was special to him. My heart will never heal from this terrible wrong to him.

I laid Tommy to rest this Friday. On this morning I was going through Tommy's poetry as a writer, quite some years ago. I found his poem called "My Time." He received an Honorable Mention for this poem in 1986 from World of Poetry. As I read this poem, his words were so profound in feeling. It was what I called his "eulogy to be."

In his honor these are his words, and I am sure when he wrote this, he never thought that some day it would be for him. I placed a copy within his ashes, as he most certainly deserves to be with God.

POLICE INVESTIGATION
November 19, 2010

The police were called that a shooting had taken place at the Palmetto Pointe Town Homes in Bluffton, South Carolina. The officers arriving at the scene saw a body lying on the ground, and a neighbor giving CPR to my son Tommy.

The police on scene had seen a person standing in the front yard. Another police officer approached the arriving officers and advised that this was the shooter.

They secured the shooter in the police car. They found his gun, a Glock, lying on the trunk of his car. He had his Miranda rights read to him. They learned his name, but he refused to talk about what had happened until he had a lawyer.

Tommy was taken to the hospital, where he died from the gunshot wound which had blown apart his chest.

The police then interviewed Lilith after they read her the Miranda rights.

Tommy wanted his garage door opener back. Lilith stated to the police that she went over to his home and entered his home (illegally). She could not find him as she walked up and down the stairs. Tommy was on his patio. When he came into his home he was startled to see Lilith. She then said he threatened her with a gun for coming into his home uninvited.

Lilith stated that she threw the door opener at the kitchen counter (not true), and then ran out of the house to tell her boyfriend what happened.

Tommy supposedly called them with threats. There is no proof of this. In fact, a police tape has Tommy calling the intrusive neighbor and saying "Are you freaking nuts?" indicating that they had been calling him incessantly. Another phone call came from Tommy, saying "I want to talk to you." Then a phone call was made by Lilith at 8:57, with no verbal message, then a phone call from Tommy at 9:03 saying, "If I do not get my door opener back, I will call the police." Clearly, she had not returned the door opener, making her statement about the visit to Tommy's house at least partially false.

When they (Lilith and Wayne) did not respond to him after that call, he went over to their house and knocked at the door. In a couple of minutes, he was dead.

In a verbal statement by Lilith to the police, she said she knew that Wayne went into the bedroom to get his gun, and she saw it in Wayne's hands as he passed her to sneak out to the garage. Then she opened the door and saw Tommy ambushed. She had a choice to stop this, but she did not.

She gave the police four different statements within a few days, which alone should justify a trial as she was the only eyewitness to the shooting. Each of the statements became a longer and longer story as to the events of what happened. First she said that Tommy took a step, and then later changed it to Tommy "lunging." Mind you, Tommy was shot from thirteen feet away. Still later, Lilith claimed that Tommy "lunged" at Wayne, who shot him "in self-defense." How could this be, when the fact is that Tommy was shot from a distance of thirteen feet?

The police asked Lilith why, if she felt threatened, did she not call 911? She said that her boyfriend "would take care of it." Well, he certainly did. He shot Tommy Mullins to death. Lilith had no reason to feel threatened, because her boyfriend was packing a Glock and Tommy Mullins was unarmed and disabled. She always felt totally comfortable in entering Tommy's home in the first place. She knew she was safe, in both homes.

The police reports and tapes contain nothing but un-truths being told by Lilith to save their backsides. And Wayne? Well, there are no tapes of Wayne. He asked for his lawyer that night and took the Fifth. Remember? I guess that's the thing to do nowadays if you want to commit murder with impunity. Shoot someone, then say they were attacking you. Have your girlfriend, who is the reason for the killing in the first place, back up the story. Then plead the Fifth as the person who pulled the trigger.

After all, the one person who could verify or deny any of Lilith's statements is dead.

Unarmed, incapacitated, and now dead, all because he wanted back something which belonged to him.

POLICE INTERVIEW OF "LILITH"

The recording of the police interview of Lilith is very revealing. The tape begins with the police questioning Lilith about why the killer would feel threatened by Tommy, a disabled man who could barely walk. Remember: if the killer was not in real danger of loss of life or of serious bodily harm when he shot Tommy Mullins, then the killer was guilty of deliberate, cold-blooded murder, or at the very least voluntary manslaughter. Lilith was the only witness, since the other person who knew the truth, Tommy Mullins, was dead.

Here is a transcript of the recording which was provided to me as mother of the murder victim. It is very difficult to listen to this recording without realizing that Lilith was trying to save her boyfriend by saying something which she knew was not true: that the killer was somehow in serious danger before shooting my unarmed son to death from thirteen feet. The transcript:

OFFICER #1 (female): "Why would he feel threatened by Tommy, who's an overweight, unhealthy guy with back problems? Why right then?"

LILITH: "Because he knew he had a gun. He knew he had a weapon."

OFFICER #1: "But what makes you think he was coming over with it?"

LILITH: "He threatened to kill him, and then there was pounding on the door."

OFFICER #1: "So you're saying he (killer) went to get the gun before the pounding on the door."

LILITH: "I'm not exactly positive on when he went to get the gun. You'd really have to ask him."

OFFICER #2 (male): "But you were there."

LILITH: "Yeah, and it really happened."

OFFICER #2: "But he's not—Tommy's not moving that fast. I mean, it's not like he RAN out of his house, and RAN to the front door and started beating on the door, so if you were in the living room, you had time to see what was going on, the telephone calls, him leaving to go get the gun...you had time to see that... you know if he...I mean you just, you had to, you had to have time to see it. He kept a gun in your bedroom?"

LILITH: "(Killer)? Yeah."

OFFICER #2: "Okay, but from that front door, if you were standing by that front door, he had to walk past you to get to the bedroom."

LILITH: "I think we were both in the living room when this was happening."

OFFICER #2: "He still had to walk past you to get to the bedroom. So when did that happen?"

LILITH: "Somewhere between the phone call and the pounding. I mean, I could try to fill it in, and, and..."

OFFICER #2: "Okay, and did that happen before, or after you called Tommy back—"

LILITH: "Honestly I don't even remember calling Tommy..."

OFFICER #2 (to someone else): "Can you show her the (records)—"

LILITH: "I know that I did."

OFFICER #3 (male): "Yeah, you did."

LILITH: "I believed you and the records, but—"

OFFICER #3: "Well, yeah, and the records wouldn't lie."

OFFICER #2: "So maybe (killer) called. Did (killer) call him back and say 'Hey look, you know, don't fucking call the house anymore, leave us alone, or else, you know'...Was it one of those?"

LILITH: "No. I don't think so. I think that it must have been me."

UNKNOWN (POSSIBLY ATTORNEY): "Timeout. Be sure of your answer. All right? You can't protect (killer). That's not our role here. So if you don't know, say you don't know."

LILITH: "I try to but he keeps—"

UNKNOWN: "Okay, but they're just trying to get to the truth. Look at me. If you don't recall calling Tommy, how many other people had access to your phone?"

LILITH: "Me and (killer)."

UNKNOWN: "So don't tell him 'No he didn't call.' If you don't know, you don't know. But when you try to say that he wouldn't have done that, or whatever...don't try to protect him and tell it a certain way. Tell him what you remember. Tell him the truth. And the truth is what you can remember, not what you think happened or what you wanted to happen, or what should happen. All right?"

OFFICER #2: "So did you call Tommy or did (killer) call Tommy?"

LILITH: "I don't know."

OFFICER #2: "Did you have your cellphone the entire time?"

LILITH: "It was on the coffee table, I think."

OFFICER #3: "Who called 911 after the shot?"

LILITH: "(Killer)."

OFFICER #3: "With what phone?"

LILITH: "His phone. I think, his phone."

OFFICER #3: "His phone?"

LILITH: "I think so."

OFFICER #1: "When he headed off to get his gun, did you know that was what he was going to do? To get his gun?"

LILITH: "I'm not sure...I, I don't know...if that's what he was gonna do or not."

OFFICER #1: "I mean, does he say anything about, 'I'm going to get my gun,' or 'You go stay here,' or 'I'm going here'? Does he give you any instructions?"

LILITH: "He just told me what Tommy had said, and when he came back he told me to get away from the door, and go to the back of the house."

OFFICER #1: "And when he said that, is there pounding on the door yet?"

LILITH: "Yeah."

OFFICER #1: "When he says that, is there already pounding at the door? He tells you what?"

LILITH: "Get away from the door, and go to the back of the house."

OFFICER #1: "And at that point, does he have a gun in his hand?"

LILITH: "Yeah."

OFFICER #1: "How long was Tommy banging on the door?"

LILITH: "Not very long. Um. Ten seconds, fifteen?"

OFFICER #1: "Before you opened the door?"

LILITH: (Silence, most likely nodding of the head in the affirmative)

OFFICER #1: "When you opened the door, does Tommy see you open the door? By the time you open it, he's already...?"

LILITH: "By the time I opened it, he's turned and going toward (killer)."

OFFICER #1: "So you didn't have an opportunity to talk to Tommy at the door."

LILITH: "No."

(Sounds of papers rustling in background)

OFFICER #3: "Is that the search warrant?"

(Unintelligible question, followed by Lilith saying "It's 1979.")

OFFICER #3: "Is there a way we can put this (Lilith's cell phone messages) on speaker phone? Oh wow. This IS an old cell phone."

LILITH: "Did that work?"

(The officers now play back the voice messages, which feature Tommy Mullins leaving messages just minutes before being killed, messages in which he expresses his desire to get his garage door opener back)

CELL PHONE: "You have three saved voice messages. To listen to your messages, press One. First saved voice message."

TOMMY MULLINS: "What are you, freakin' nuts? You need to come over here and I want to talk to you. Call me back. Bye."

CELL PHONE: "End of message. To erase this message, press Seven. To save it, press Nine. To hear more options, press Zero. To replay this message, press Four. To get envelope information about this message, press Five. Sent Friday November 19th at 8:55 PM from phone number 843-227-1953. Duration 14 seconds. To erase this message, press Seven. To save it, press Nine. To hear more options. This message will be saved for 21 days. Next message.

TOMMY MULLINS: "If you do not bring my garage door opener back right now, I will call the police and have them come on over to get it."

CELL PHONE: "End of message. To erase this message, press Seven. To save it, press Nine. To hear more options, press Zero. To replay this message, press Four. To get envelope information about this message, press Five. Sent Friday November 19th at 9:03 pm"

(Note to reader: Six minutes later, Tommy was dead.)

OFFICER #3: "Now I'm more confused. At 9:03 he said 'Bring it here or I'm going to call the police' and then suddenly he shows up banging at the door with his garage door opener in his pocket." (Note to reader: This is very problematic for the defense in a trial, because the garage door opener was apparently found in Tommy's pocket at the murder scene. Why would he come over right after leaving a message to return the opener or he would call the police? He would come over to get the opener. It would appear to a logical person that the garage door opener was put into his pocket before the police arrived.)

OFFICER #1: "Now, his coat's back at the house. He's not wearing the coat when he shows up."

OFFICER #2: "Yeah. His coat was at the house."

OFFICER #3: "So if he's threatening to call the police, it just doesn't make sense for him to come over and bang on the door."

OFFICER #1: "Unless he somehow found it and he's coming over to tell them, but that...no, I'm totally lost. Because that's the last phone call, right?"

OFFICER #3: "Right? 9:03."

OFFICER #3: "Unless the 911 call...When was the 911 call?"

OFFICER #1: "That's (Tommy's last phone call at 9:03) AFTER he's already talked to (killer)."

OFFICER #3: "9:09. 9:09 when we got dispatched. Literally six minutes later."

OFFICER #1: "So as soon as he made that call he came over."

OFFICER #3: "Absolutely. It makes no sense."

OFFICER #1: "Have you ever had any episodes with him like that before, where he does things that make no sense? Has he been threatening before?"

LILITH: "One time he, um, he was really drunk and I went over there and he was talking about some drug dealers that had ripped him off, in Spartanburg or New Jersey or somewhere, that he was gonna make a phone call and have them taken care of, and he was talking crazy and I emailed or texted one of my friends and said stay away from him because he was crazy. So yeah he did sometimes say crazy shit."

OFFICER #3: "What? Where in those messages does he make a threat in any way? As a matter of fact, the only threat he makes, if you want to call it a threat, is when he says he'll call the police. So how do you go from those messages, and somewhere in those messages, I mean, I don't think it was the last call. That was the message he left. So he must have called (killer) before that. Okay, so if he calls (killer) and threatens (killer) that he going to effing kill him, and then he calls afterwards and says 'I'm going to call the police.' Where is that threat level? Okay. I can understand if he says 'I'm going to effing kill you and then comes over and bangs on the door, but he doesn't. He talks to (killer) first, then may have said, 'I'm going to effing kill you,' but then he calls back and he leaves a message, saying 'I'm going to call the police.' So at what point does (killer) decide that this is such a huge threat that he's going to go get his gun?"

LILITH: "(killer) probably didn't know that he had called back at that point."

OFFICER #3: "Well, it will show up on your phone that he's calling."

LILITH: "But he didn't know what he said, I would think, at that point."

OFFICER #2: "Did (killer) call Tom and threaten Tom? Or when Shane called Tom, is that when Tom said, 'Look'—

LILITH: "Tommy called us, and that's when he threatened—"

OFFICER #3: "This is what I think. That one phone call that was placed to Tom's was made by (killer). Right? From your phone? You didn't call (killer). You don't remember because you didn't make that phone call. Wayne did. Isn't that right?"

LILITH: "Hm-mmm. I mean, I don't remember if he did or

48

not. I don't think though, that he did."

OFFICER #3: "It was either you or (killer)."

OFFICER #2: "And it wasn't you."

OFFICER #3: "When you say you don't think you did, that taints what you're saying."

LILITH: "Well, I could say I made the phone call, but I don't remember making it."

OFFICER #3: "Well then, just say that. Don't say you think or don't think; just say what you know."

LILITH: "Okay. I know that I don't remember if I made the phone call or not."

OFFICER #3: "Do you remember calling Tom and saying 'I told (killer) what happened?' And that's why he called back and said, 'What are you, freaking nuts?' What were you nuts about?"

LILITH: "Probably, I, I don't remember what was going through Tommy's mind. I wish the toxicology was back, so that would explain a little bit more if he was plastered or..."

OFFICER #3: "Well, whether he was plastered or not, and possibly he was, but, and probably he was plastered, but still at one point you do something to make him think that you're effing nuts. What is it that you do that makes him think that you're nuts?"

LILITH: "Probably it was that I ran out of there, and he started calling."

OFFICER #3: "Someone running out of the house I wouldn't consider nuts, if they're having a gun thrown at them."

OFFICER #2: "I think Tommy was upset that you was in his house without his permission. And you probably was going through his medications, and that—"

LILITH: "Give me a lie detector test. And I'll answer it. I wasn't stealing anything."

OFFICER #2: "I'm trying to figure out why would he say 'Are you effing nuts?' If you didn't talk on the phone, he wouldn't have reason to say 'Are you effing nuts?'. But if he found you in the house, after—"

LILITH: "I was always in his house."

OFFICER #2: "But on this particular day, he was trying to cut it off."

LILITH: "I don't know."

OFFICER #1: "If he had just come in from being out walking his dog and put his gun on the table, could you have overreacted to seeing the gun, and he thought that was effing nuts?"

LILITH: "I know he pointed it at me."

OFFICER #1: "He pointed it at you? The barrel was pointed at—"

LILITH: "At my...chest area."

OFFICER #1: "And did he say anything when he pointed it at you?"

LILITH: "I think I thought at that point, 'You're fucking crazy' and I ran out."

OFFICER #1: "But he didn't say anything, or he didn't answer to that, or—"

LILITH: "I think I ran pretty fast out of there."

OFFICER #1: "You didn't hear him yelling at you?"

LILITH: "No."

OFFICER #3: "I just, I'm dumbfounded by these messages. Neither one of them, I mean, if Tommy is in this rage, that both you and (killer) portray him to be in, neither one of those messages are threatening. These other messages that he left are deleted from your phone. I'm not sure what they said. But I bet they could probably help us out with what happened. Did you purposely delete those?"

LILITH: "I think I deleted some messages, yeah."

OFFICER #2: "What did they say?"

LILITH: "I don't remember."

OFFICER #3: "Did you purposely delete them to cover for (killer)?"

LILITH: "No. No."

OFFICER #3: "Why would you delete those, and not—"

LILITH: "Probably it had something to do with drugs."

OFFICER #2: "Like I asked earlier, did Tom, did he believe you was in his house looking for drugs? Not saying you stole, but the messages when he called you back or whenever he confronted you in the house, is that was he was thinking? Did he say anything about that?"

LILITH: "No."

OFFICER #2: "Well then why would he leave you a message, possibly about drugs, then? And then you erased them? That would make sense to me. And like we already talked about, we don't care about the drugs. But what would make sense is if you was in his house, and he thought you was looking for drugs..."

LILITH: "He may have thought that."

OFFICER #2: "Okay. He may have. And then when he called you back on the phone and left those first couple of messages, that you believe are about drugs, well then, that makes sense for him to call you back and say 'Why are you in my house?' or 'Why are you looking for the drugs?' or whatever. And now you erase those messages, thinking we care about that, when we really don't. Okay? Now that makes sense. For you just to up and erase them, and leave these two, when all he is saying is he wants his stuff back or he is gonna call the cops, you know, calling asking you about 'What are you doing in the house?' or about the drugs, that's not threatening. Okay. In any messages about those drugs, I don't think he was threatening you. He wasn't threatening you in those messages, was he?"

LILITH: "I don't remember those messages. I really don't remember every single thing or recall, and..."

OFFICER #2: "But you do recall it being about drugs?"

LILITH: "I think so."

OFFICER #1: "What was the gist of those phone calls?"

LILITH: "You know, I really need a cigarette. Can I have one?"

OFFICER #1: "As soon as you answer that question. That'll answer a lot of stuff. What was the gist of those phone calls? What was he really pissed about? Because he—"

LILITH: "About getting fucked up in Ridgeland."

OFFICER #1: "And so he said stuff about that?"

LILITH: "Yeah, he said 'Why do you keep fucking up?'"

There is a long silence.

OFFICER #1: "Why does he care so much?"

OFFICER #3: "You can remember what these messages say, but you can't remember who called him back? You can remember specific details about him lunging towards (killer), but you can't remember if you called him back on your phone?"

LILITH: "I can't remember calling him."

OFFICER #3: "I'm not saying you."

LILITH: "I don't remember."

OFFICER #3: "You remember everything else, every detail."

LILITH: "I don't think I did so great with details."

OFFICER #3: "Oh, it's fairly detailed, you know. You're telling us specific details about the incident, but one specific one, that I think anybody would know, is who made the phone call back to him. If he's calling bothering you all—"

LILITH: "I wish I could ask (killer) right now, if he made the call."

OFFICER #3: "Well, if you don't remember doing it, then..."

LILITH: "I don't remember if he called him."

OFFICER #3: "Do you remember (killer) grabbing the phone from you?

LILITH: "I remember (killer) answering the phone."

OFFICER #3: "Are you sure he answered the phone, and didn't dial it?"

LILITH: "There was one call and he answered it."

OFFICER #3: "Are you sure? He answered it, and didn't dial it?"

LILITH: "Because it was ringing, yeah."

OFFICER #1: "I don't have any more questions."

OFFICER #3: "No, me either."

OFFICER #1: "I'm not sure what else to ask. I think we're covered."

OFFICER #3: "Is there something we didn't ask you which you think is important?"

LILITH: "My head is spinning right now."

UNKNOWN PERSON (MALE), POSSIBLY ATTORNEY: "Well, why don't you go get a cigarette and then come back, and I want you to think through everything and then tell them what they forgot to ask you. If you think it's important. Because you're the one who was there. They weren't there. I just think the more open you can be, the most information you can give them, the better off you will be. As you know, I don't give a damn about your husband. I mean, I do on a personal level, but where we are here legally I don't. You know, that's not your responsibility or mine. I think (Lilith) has a tremendous sense of guilt, and I think that she is very affectionate toward Tommy. You're very affectionate toward what's his name (killer), and she feels that she's the one that caused this. I mean, that's what you've told her. And I think that she thinks that her drug use is what caused this, and she has tremendous guilt about that, but what I want to be sure of is that her guilt is not protecting anybody from something that they may be responsible for. In defense of you, (Lilith)..."

LILITH: "I just feel like if I had never would have been involved in drugs, or...it's stupid."

UNKNOWN: "Well, you did do some stupid things. But that doesn't excuse other people's stupid things. And if you have anything else to add, it's critical that you do it now. You can't get in trouble for anything you've said today. Nothing. Zero. And if you didn't say something today, and they find out about it later, you can get in trouble, and all this is for naught, all this angst, emotion, (unintelligible) screaming at us, all of it, all the rest of it, okay, all I want is to get closure today. That's what I said to you and to your dad. I want you to be able to walk out of here and not forget what happened, not be in fear, that...and that if you're absolutely..."

LILITH: "I've been honest."

UNKNOWN: "But have you been completely honest? Is there anything that they didn't ask you that you know is important?"

LILITH: "Can I think about it?"

UNKNOWN: "Well, go and have a cigarette and think about it."

END OF INTERVIEW

As you can see from this interview, the phone evidence shows that Tommy made no threat toward the killer or his girlfriend, and the physical evidence shows that Tommy was both unarmed and not close enough or able enough to harm the killer. Yet, he was shot to death anyway. Lilith later took the Fifth Amendment in order to avoid incriminating herself, as did the killer, and they were not available for testimony as a result.

NOTE: The night of Tommy's murder, according to the dated police report November 19, 2010 and signed, that evening the police confiscated many items from Tommy's home. There was no mention that a garage door opener was found.

THE MURDER

The murder took an instant.

Cause of death: Heart, lung and esophagus perforations, due to a penetrating gunshot wound to the chest.

The weapon: a .40-caliber firearm known as a Glock.

My God. My son, Tommy, was blown apart.

It is important, in looking at the events which preceded the murder of my son, to keep in mind that Lilith had offered to take Tommy's dog, Rocky, for walks while Tommy was away for his back surgery. This offer served to get Tommy's guard down about Lilith's real motive for dog-walking: access to Tommy's house.

When Tommy later felt that his back had recovered enough to walk Rocky, he asked for his garage door opener back. Initially, she gave it back, but caused Tommy distress by crying about it, and by emailing Tommy with messages like "WHY ARE YOU DOING THIS? ALL I WANT TO DO IS WALK ROCKY!" These messages and her emotional protests worked. Tommy gave in. Once more, she had the door opener back. And then things began to get complicated, problematic and, eventually, out of hand.

Tommy was now on medications for pain, and now Lilith was sneaking into his home to steal them. Tommy spoke with his sister about it, and she suggested he get a lock box. He did, but it did not solve anything, as Lilith continued entering his home unannounced. It was becoming more than just a problem. He spoke with his pastor about the subject, saying he was trying to break away from a friend but without success.

Tommy said that Lilith had a sister in jail, and he didn't want to make things even worse for her family. Tommy was like that. He didn't want to bring harm to others, even to others who might bring harm to him.

Sadly, Tommy's desire not to bring harm to Lilith or her

family led to his own death.

In text messages retained by the police, Tommy told Lilith to leave him alone. When Lilith was interviewed by the police, she said she did go back into his house that night, but only to give Tommy his door opener back. Once again, she entered his home without permission, and the telephone evidence shows that she did not enter for the purpose of giving back the opener. How do we, and the police, know this? Because at 9:03 pm, in response to an 8:57 pm call from Lilith, Tommy left this message on her voicemail: "Are you freaking nuts?" And then another message: "If I do not get my garage door opener back, I will call the police." These messages are in the interview in the preceding chapter of this book.

Six minutes later, Tommy was dead.

Clearly Tommy decided, after hanging up the phone, to go to their house and knock on the door to get the opener back. There is no law against such a normal action. There is, however, a law against murdering someone for taking such a normal action. Tommy was well within his rights in seeking the return of his property, visiting his neighbors unarmed and for that singular purpose.

Later you will see that a trial never occurred. Three crucial questions which a jury should have been asked to consider: Why did Lilith and Wayne not call the police if they felt threatened? Why did Wayne come out of the house unnecessarily? And why did he shoot a man who was just standing there, unarmed?

After Tommy was shot, a neighbor became aware of the commotion. His dogs were barking, alerting him to the events outside. The neighbor opened his door and saw Tommy lying on the ground. The neighbor ran to him, and started CPR, which he continued until the ambulance arrived. By this time, Tommy was near death. Lilith then came and stood over Tommy, saying "I am sorry, Tommy."

My God. How can someone be responsible for another person's death, at least indirectly as Lilith was, and then offer a feeble and insincere apology minutes after her boyfriend has murdered her neighbor essentially on her behalf?

Three years later, I learned that Lilith tried to kill herself with a gun, only to miss her heart. At the same time, the killer's car has many stickers pasted on it. One of them says, "I am a bitter gun owner." As if something bad happened to him because he owned a gun! No. Something bad and very final happened to my son because the killer owned a gun for the purpose of ambush and murder.

Wayne will have to answer in God's Court. Karma will be in attendance.

THE BAIL HEARING

After only twelve days in jail, the killer appeared in court for the bail hearing.

The state of South Carolina provides what is called an advocate. He or she is to assist the victim's family in all that will be happening for any court appearances involving the killer and the trial. I was notified the day before that on the twelfth day of the killer's incarceration, the advocate would pick me up at my home at eight a.m. for the drive to Beaufort and the Beaufort County courthouse, for the bail hearing. The hearing was scheduled for nine a.m.

Well, she never arrived. It was now nearing 8:30. I called her, and she said "I'm on my way." Finally, she arrived, and we still had the 45-minute drive to Beaufort.

Driving into the courthouse complex to find a parking spot was all taking time, and for sure we were going to be late.

Shaking and distraught, I was directed by the advocate through the courthouse doors. To enter a courtroom, you have to pass through a machine that checks your body and pocketbook for devices which you should not be carrying. Then a wand is passed over your body.

The wand made a noise, a crazy noise that made me think something was wrong with me. I felt panicked. What was going on? Well, it turned out to be my knees setting off the alarms. I had surgery on both of them, and the metal that was inserted into my knees created the false alarm at the courthouse. As if I wasn't already upset enough! I did not need to add that panicked, terrified emotion to my turmoil on this day or any other.

The advocate needed to look for the correct courtroom, and we rushed down the cold halls of marble. Finding the courtroom which would hold the bail hearing, I heard her say, "Here it is!" We had made it just in time.

I started shaking almost uncontrollably. We entered the

room, and the advocate said we needed to sit in particular seats. My shaking had become unbearable, as I did not know what was to come about. The icy-cold courtroom only added to my distress.

After I sat down, the advocate told me not to look up, because they were bringing in the killer. But I could not imagine being able to sit through the entire hearing without looking at the evil man who gunned down my son in cold blood.

The killer's lawyer stood before the judge and made a statement, which seemed to be filled with sentiments designed to get the judge to feel sympathy for Wayne. The lawyer's goal was to get the judge to set a killer free on bond, and for the bond to not be too expensive. Unfortunately, the lawyer succeeded.

The judge allowed the murderer to go free on bail of just $7,500, representing ten percent of $75,000. The lawyer was hired by Lilith's father, who was paying his daughter's boyfriend's legal expenses.

The judge asked the killer whether or not he had a job. "Yes," said the killer. Then the judge ordered the killer to stay in the state of South Carolina at all times. He could not leave the state or the country, for he had killed a man. The judge also ordered the killer to go straight home after work every day until the trial.

And then a shocking thing happened.

The judge ordered the killer to live in his girlfriend's parents' home, which is right down the street from my house. The murderer of my son would be living down the street from the mother of his victim! The insensitivity of the judge to the emotional distress which this would cause for me was staggering. The judge then had the nerve to say to me, "If you see the killer drive by your home or approach your house, please let us know."

Well, I have to tell you, I wasn't going to sit by my window and look for the killer. The truth is that there is no way he should have been free on bond in the first place, much less to be ordered to live as my neighbor, for heaven's sake.

The killer was instructed not to come within a thousand feet of me personally. I wanted to say, "Wow. Thanks a lot...how about a million feet?" But I kept my composure, still in disbelief that he was getting out on such inexpensive bond.

The killer was ordered to take the back way out of the neighborhood instead of driving by my house when going to work. And then the killer was free to go.

Free to go. I think about those words a lot. If the killer had simply pointed his gun at Tommy, and said, "We disagree about your garage door opener, Tommy, but you're free to go," my son would be alive today. Instead, I must live with the absence of my son in the world, and "Free to go" is what the killer gets.

But at least there would be the trial. Thank goodness, there would be the trial. I had to be patient. Let the justice system carry out justice its way. After the trial, the killer would never be a free man again. That would not bring Tommy back, but would be justice, and would show the appropriate respect for the value of my innocent son's life.

I was not allowed to speak up at this hearing. Even when the killer smirked at me, which chilled me to the bone, I was forced to keep silent. I was told to stay in my seat until the killer had exited the courtroom, so I did. But I will never forget that smirk. It said, "Yeah, lady, I killed your son, and I would do it again." It was that kind of look, that indicated that he thought it was funny that Tommy was dead. Of course, when a man has numerous "badass" bumper stickers on the back of his car about the Second Amendment and his precious gun rights, it is no surprise when he is eager to use a gun to kill somebody. Any excuse would do. His excuse was a weak one: "self-defense." What a laugh, except that it's not funny at all.

When the prosecutor came over to speak with me, all I could do was cry. Through my tears, I told the prosecutor that I could not understand why a confessed killer would not be behind bars until his trial.

Needless to say, I wasn't the only resident of our neighborhood to be upset that the killer would be living amongst us. Many families were furious, and some people even purchased and installed security systems and hired security companies to monitor their homes. I even heard of a petition being circulated, to demand that the killer not be allowed to live in our community.

How could a judge be so cruel? What a slap in the face, to assign a killer to be living down the street from his victim's mother. The community was up in arms as well, and rightfully so. We all had to endure the knowledge that a killer was living among us.

I started writing letters to the court, citing how horrible and insensitive a decision that was on the judge's part. Finally, I was heard. After about three months, the killer was ordered to move back in with his girlfriend in the community where my son had lived...and where my son was killed. "Pick your poison," I guess they say.

Some weeks later, I received a phone call from the advocate, telling me that the prosecutor would not be handling the case, and that a new prosecutor had been assigned.

AFTER THE BAIL HEARING

At the bail hearing after Wayne was charged with murdering my son, as Wayne was leaving the courtroom, he turned to me with this evil sneer, then smirked, looking straight into my eyes, as if to say, "Yeah, I got your son."

I was devastated. IT IS SO HARD TO COMPREHEND THE EVIL IN A PERSON.

Now, with Wayne walking free, I had to wait for a trial, knowing nothing about our justice system, and with nothing being explained to me. It was so confusing.

The next thing to happen was I received from the State of South Carolina a memo asking for the cost of Tommy's burial. Yes, the state reimburses for burial, as compensation for the death of a person who is a victim. We, the family, will always be victims.

It is called the South Carolina Victims Assistance program. This is a program designed to help victims with expenses directly resulting from a crime, and which are not covered by other payment sources.

Let's see here: the state gave me money...oh, but that money is part of my taxes, and the killer did not have to contribute to any of this, certainly not out of his pocket for the murder he committed. This just does not make sense to me.

If counseling is needed, including lost wages, they cover up to $4,000. Of course this was greatly appreciated, but again a killer seems to have special privileges in the justice system. Wayne had to endure nothing, and had to pay nothing.

We wished this never happened. My son alive was what was needed. His life was taken, robbed, by a senseless murder. As Clint Eastwood's character, William Munny, said in *Unforgiven*, "It's a hell of a thing, killing a man. You take away everything he has, and everything he's ever going to have."

THOUGHTS FOR AN OPEN SHERIFF'S MEETING

I prepared the following speech for an open meeting of the Sheriff's office:

I am here this evening to listen to what you have to say, being that you are the sheriff. I am on a mission for my son tonight, and I want to say sadly that my son was murdered this past November by a neighbor.

What infuriates me is that this guy was let out on bail of just $7500 and allowed to live down the street from me. What a slap in the face this was, but finally after many complaints he was moved back to where the murder took place, to live with his girlfriend. Can you imagine two people living with each other after such a horrid crime was committed by one of them, and they go on living as if they did nothing wrong?

This is such insanity. To think a killer walks among us, enjoying the fruits of life while my son is dead, and that as time goes by the case has not even come up to the grand jury, as it is always being postponed. Why, I ask? Why??? No one tells me.

It boggles my mind trying to understand that when a person has admitted to the crime of murder, he is not left in jail until the trial comes about.

All I hear is "This guy has rights!" WHAT? I scream. Where are my son's rights? This guy took them away when he shot Tommy. My son was unarmed, and not in this man's home.

The killer took matters into his own hands. He thought he had a right to kill my son. A gun, it seems, makes a person feel in power. He just wanted my son dead.

Now our country wants an easing of gun laws. This is also insane, as you can imagine it will probably become the Old West out there, where if somebody looks at you funny, out will come the guns. You just shoot them. That was the thinking of the killer who took everything from my son and from me.

I want justice for my son, who has no say in what happens or happened. This guy took away my son's rights to live and to pursue happiness.

My son was a good person, and he was so happy that he was about to start playing drums in his church that following Sunday. But this guy murdered him on Friday, so on Sunday, instead of watching and listening to the joy of my son's music, I had his wake. This has been such sadness for me and for my family, and we pray that this killer will get what he deserves. One way or another.

I did not get to deliver this speech that night, because it turned out that the only topic being discussed was immigration. I was sad that I could not have my say at an open meeting, but decided to keep these words anyway. I even mailed this speech to the sheriff.

THE CASTLE HEARING

T
he next event to take place was the Castle Hearing. I was notified of the date and time to be there, and then I called family members so they could make arrangements to attend this hearing.

A feeling of gut sickness was all I felt as we watched them bring in the killer. We all sat close together shoulder-to-shoulder, keeping each of us from harm from what was to be said as to why the killer should get off without any punishment.

Our family found the Castle Hearing to be very upsetting. The defense wanted to get the killer off on the Castle Law, which says that a killer has the right to kill a person if he feels that he or someone else is in danger. It was a sickening feeling, to listen to them argue that the killer felt in some way endangered by Tommy to the point of committing homicide.

They even had "witnesses." One was an ex-policeman from New York City, who said terrible things about Tommy, and said that he did not think that Tommy was mentally qualified to have a gun, and that Tommy often had asked him to go shooting at the range for practice. My question: What in the world is wrong with Tommy asking someone to go target shooting with him at the range? Tommy legally owned a gun and a permit, and would at times join a neighbor to go on such outings.

During four hours of excruciating argument and testimony, the defense used the Big Bad Wolf as an analogy. I'm not joking. They really did. The Big Bad Wolf. As if Tommy was somehow a wolf breaking down his neighbors' door, looking for defenseless pigs. This argument was ludicrous. A disabled man knocking on a neighbor's door to retrieve his garage door opener is not analogous to the story of the Big Bad Wolf. It was an absurd four hours, let me tell you.

A tape was given to the judge during the hearing. The girlfriend and the killer said they had received a "verbal threat" from Tommy, saying he was going to "fucking kill them." There was no recording of Tommy saying such a thing. Just the killer and the girlfriend saying that Tommy had threatened them on the phone. But interestingly, the killer and girlfriend had deleted all but two phone messages from Tommy, neither of which indicated the slightest threat from Tommy. Logic asks this question: "If Tommy made a threatening phone call, why did you delete it after killing Tommy?" The answer: they wouldn't delete it. So they claimed that Tommy made the threat on the phone in a live conversation...but two recorded messages right before Tommy was murdered reveal Tommy asking if the girlfriend is crazy and repeating the request to get his garage door opener back. Hence, no proof existed, whatsoever, that Tommy threatened them in any way.

The judge apparently felt the same way, that there was no proof at all that the killer and his girlfriend were in danger. Since Tommy also wasn't trying to break into their home, they had no case under the Castle Doctrine. The defense's request for dismissal of the case under Castle Law was denied.

There is an excellent article in *Bluffton Today,* dated July 29, 2011, reporting the judge's decision to deny the Castle Law request by the defense. It is available online via Google. Just type "Thomas Mullins, Jr." and "Bluffton Today," or the title of the article: **Judge Denies Motion to Dismiss Manslaughter Charge.**

After the Castle hearing, all we did was wait and wait, with me still writing letters including "Justice Delayed, Justice Denied." This system of justice is terrible. It gives a killer rights which far exceed those of victims and victims' families. Nobody seems to care about victims in this system. One feels absolutely alone.

FUN WITH THE POLAROID CAMERA

Donna, Tommy, Lenny, Patti.

EASTER

Lenny, Russ, Tommy, Donna and Patti.

A DAY AT THE BEACH

Donna, Tommy, Mom, Lenny and Patti.

MARCHING IN THE PARADE

DAY AT THE PARK

Donna, Tommy, Lenny
and Patti.

Patti, Mom, Lenny, Tommy
and Donna

CHRISTMAS

Tommy, Mom, Grandma, Patti and Jingles

ANOTHER EASTER

Patti, Lenny, Donna and Tommy.

FAMILY PORTRAIT

Tom, Joan, Patti, Donna, Lenny and Tommy.

KINDERGARTEN

HIGH SCHOOL GRADUATION

SHANNON AND UNCLE TOM

Miss you Uncle Tom,
I will always remember when you showed me how to make the
best recipe for eggplant parmesan. And when in college we had
some fun times hanging out.

Love,
Shannon

TOMMY ESCORTING MOM FOR HIS SISTER'S WEDDING

Joan C. Mullins

ANOTHER CHRISTMAS

TOMMY THE POET

TOMMY...SO HANDSOME

TOMMY IN FLORIDA

FUN DAY WITH FAMILY AND FRIENDS

Mom, Tommy, Shannon, Nephew Tommy, Donna, TJ, Med and Ruthie.

FINALLY HERE

LIVING IN BLUFFTON

A VISIT FROM KATIE

TOMMY IN SAVANNAH, GA

MOM, KATIE AND TOMMY

CHARLESTON VISIT
&
PIZZA

DADDY'S LITTLE GIRL

A DAY OUT FOR PIZZA

A FAMILY GET TOGETHER

TOMMY LOVED GOING TO OUTBACK FOR HIS FAVORITE HAMBURGERS

FOREVER BEST FRIENDS

Rocky and Tommy

MIRA AND WINSTON

ROCKY WITH PUMPKIN

ROCKY AND MIRA

ROCKY AND MIRA, CONTINUED

KISSES FOR KATIE

A SURPRISE FROM ROCKY
JUMPING ON MY LAP

TRIP TO THE "MOON"

Tommy's surprise birthday party with his buddies from New Jersey

Joan C. Mullins

TRIP TO THE "MOON"

PARTY
GUYS

TOMMY'S 50TH BIRTHDAY

TOMMY'S LAST PICTURE

Tommy became a member of the church this day.
He was murdered five days later.

MONTHLY BEAUTIFUL FLOWERS SAYING "THANK YOU, MOM!"

A CARD FROM TOMMY

The caption of this card is:

"YOU DID IT!
The stars have written your name across the sky
...celebrating amazing you"

Thoughtful and with Love, Tommy gave me this card after he watched two of my children's books performed as a lovely ballet dance on Hilton Head Island in May of 2010. Sadly he was murdered six months later.

DEAR MOM,

I AM So proud OF
OF ALL you Did, you
have come So FAR +
ALL your Hard work has
Paid ofF, YOUR A STAR!
IN the FACE OF the SKy

CAPTURe your moment
ANd wrap It AROUNd your
HeArt, It's A Memorie that
will Live oN Forever, IN Time
Great work! Love your
                    SON
                    Tommy

...celebrating amazing you.

CONGRATULATIONS

TOMMY, I MISS YOU SO.
EVERY DAY IS A HEARTACHE.

THANK YOU FOR BEING
A WONDERFUL SON.

MY LOVE IS WITH YOU FOREVER.

A NEWS ARTICLE FEATURING TOMMY

T he following article appeared in The Island Packet in April of 2009, seven months before Tommy was murdered. In the article, Tommy is revealed as the good citizen he was, looking out for the neighborhood along with his loyal dog, Rocky. Note that Tommy is pictured on his regular walk with Rocky, and that he did not carry anything around with him on these walks...neither gun nor alcohol nor anything but Rocky's leash. This article even shows the selflessness which Tommy possessed, as he helped prevent thieves from stealing from homes which were still in progress. Here is the article, by Jay Karr of The Island Packet:

BUILDER ABANDONED DEVELOPMENT, PALMETTO POINTE TOWNES RESIDENTS SAY
By JOSH McCANN. jmccann@islandpacket.com. 843-706-8145
JAY KARR/THE ISLAND PACKET
April 7, 2009

Palmetto Pointe resident Tom Mullins and his dog Rocky have had to drive thieves away from these townhomes that have sat uncompleted for nine months since builder Portrait Homes halted construction at the half-finished development off S.C. 46 near Pritchardville. In addition, homeowners are no longer receiving landscaping services, termite prevention or pool maintenance for which they've paid. They've also had problems getting warranty issues taken care of.

First, residents of Palmetto Pointe Townes in Bluffton couldn't get warranty claims addressed by the builder, they said.

Then, the residents said, the neighborhood's homeowners association, controlled by builder Pasquinelli & Portrait Homes,

stopped providing many services their dues were supposed to cover.

Now, two buildings in the neighborhood have been left unfinished. Construction stopped months ago, and the buildings have attracted animals and thieves, the residents said.

Town officials have posted signs declaring the structures unsafe.

Dirt bikes and all-terrain vehicles run through the neighborhood's vacant land.

The neighborhood's travails have some homeowners concerned about their property values and considering legal action, resident Michelle Harrigan said.

"We are stuck," she said. "The only recourse we have is a lawsuit."

Jonathan Dedmon, a spokesman for the builder, said the company is selling existing homes in many of its communities but is not breaking ground on new ones. He said he could not immediately answer questions about the unfinished buildings or the residents' other concerns.

The neighborhood was to include 120 townhomes, priced from $140,0000 on up, near the intersection of S.C. 46 and S.C. 170, Harrigan said. Other than models used to sell the property, only 20 units have been built and 18 are occupied, she said.

Harrigan bought a unit in the neighborhood in July. After

months of research, she said, she saw no signs of trouble.

Since she moved in, an improperly installed back door has allowed spiders and a snake inside.

"Every single one of us have warranty issues that have not been touched," she said.

The builder's representatives have pledged to fix problems, but they have missed appointments without rescheduling them, residents said.

In addition, the homeowners association hasn't provided landscaping, termite services or pool care as promised, Harrigan said.

Instead, a group of residents volunteered to tend to the pool.

Tom Mullins was among the first to move to the neighborhood in late 2007.

Since then, he and his dog, a boxer named Rocky, have kept an eye on the unfinished buildings as the neighborhood has deteriorated.

Looking at the dying plants in a parking lot median, Mullins lamented how pretty they once looked.

Pointing to his unit, he said he plans to stay at least until the housing market picks up again.

He doesn't expect to find any buyers unless the neighborhood's condition improves.

"I know I'm not going to be able to sell it," he said.

AUTHOR'S NOTE: *This community has since recovered very nicely, which is a compliment to the homeowners and the builders. –Joan*

SECOND PROSECUTOR
AND THIRD PROSECUTOR

The first prosecutor decided prior to the Castle Hearing to retire. I now had a number-two prosecutor. The meeting with this man turned into an uncomfortable situation . We tried to ask questions, and his personality turned to annoyed. His words and attitude were saying, "I am in charge here." Maybe so, but we had rights also to ask anything, as we are victims, but he just put us down.

He began by telling us he would not have taken this case if he did not think he could get a conviction. He believed that Tommy was ambushed, and said he felt that he would make sure the killer was looking at jail time of double digits.

"How long will it be before a trial?" we asked. "Maybe two years," he replied. Of course we became upset, as we are victims also and the killer has the privilege of going on with his life.

We have no control over the system, but a prosecutor can be the one in charge of wanting a swift trial. It was at his discretion, but this did not happen.

I had been writing to the Solicitor who was in charge of the 14th district, telling him about my son and all pertaining to Tommy's handicaps, and how we felt that the killer was still out and about enjoying his life while we were suffering as victims.

He told me to stop writing letters because he did not like this; mind you, he was trying to take my freedom of speech from me. I kept writing letters though, and I did not care if he did not like this. I had to say how I felt.

But the good news from the Castle Hearing meant that the trial would go forth, and that was my focus.

One year went by, then into the second year. Was there ever going to be a trial? we asked, and then the phone call finally came. A trial date had been set for August 2012.

All of a sudden I received another phone call to tell me the trial had to be postponed because two witnesses were going to be out of town and could not get back for the trial.

So once again we had to wait, but to our surprise we were notified that another court date was set for September, only one month later. Finally we were filled with hopes and prayers that Tommy would find justice.

We just wanted to get this trial over with, and had faith that the prosecutor would deliver, and hoped he would be able to hold up to his words that he would see that the killer received jail time in "double digits."

Two weeks before the trial, the killer asked for a bond reduction. I was notified to go to court and was told I could have my say. When I got to the courthouse, my prosecutor told me that not only did they want the bond reduced, but the killer was also asking to travel into Georgia to work.

Why go into Georgia? He already had a job in Bluffton. He had special restrictions from the bail hearing of how his life was going to be, but he wanted more freedom. That's all. Why should he be awarded anything he wants?

My prosecutor had told me beforehand that the killer would be granted this request, but this did not sink into my mind until the hearing progressed, and not before I was ushered up to the judge to have my say. I was so nervous that all I can remember saying was that I felt that the killer should not be given any rights. I was then ushered off of the podium and was told to wait in the back of the courtroom.

As I was walking back, the judge yelled out "Oh thank you Ms. Mullins."

How very rude of this judge to yell this out, and so embarrassing. Where was the judge's courtesy to speak to me while I was still standing by the bench, knowing the pain I must be in from Tommy's murder.

The courtroom filled with prisoners and spectators, all staring at me.

Before the defense spoke that the killer was not present today, my prosecutor stood up, saying "Ms. Mullins does not like the way the killer looks at her, so I said for him to stay away." What right had he to do this? Where was the defense to have a say in this? Of course you know this was all planned.

My prosecutor by law was to be telling me everything that was to go on, and not wait until the last minute. My rights as a victim according to legal paperwork were taken away from me. This information was sent to me by the Justice Department on "Victims' Rights."

I should have been asked about the killer being present or not, regardless of how I felt when he looked at me. It was my choice, not my prosecutor's decision.

The defense lawyer got up to have his say about the bond, and all that had to be said to the judge to help the judge make a decision about whether or not to allow the killer to get what is being asked.

Next my prosecutor had his say. Now he was to be on our side, but what came out of his mouth was startling. Every time I needed to see the killer, he would be available to me (I was never told of these meetings). He said some other short remarks. Now I am thinking, "What is this man doing? He is not on our side, when out of his mouth comes 'I feel that the killer is not a threat to the community.'"

What! I am screaming in my head. *What in God's name is he saying? This guy killed my son and he is NOT a threat to society?*

Of course with that statement the killer got, once again, special privileges from our justice system, and now was granted the right to leave the state without restrictions.

I wanted to go home, as I was so in shock, but the advocate ushered me into a small room off of the courtroom. I was not to leave, as the prosecutor wanted to talk with me.

Here he came, saying to me "Well, we had half a win." What in the heck was he telling me? What was he meaning? I was never given an explanation. He had used this phrase before. And his attitude frightened me, as he could see the look on my face for sure.

He then sat down. I started asking him some questions about some of the facts I had read in the police report, that the girlfriend had no right to be in my son's home that night, as he specifically told her to stay away from him and Rocky, his dog. This was hours before he was killed.

The prosecutor threw his head back in a laughing gesture. He did this all the time. My God, what was this man doing? He most certainly had taken my son out of the picture, and it was now well apparent that he was on the side of the killer.

I started asking more questions. He started to yell and scream at me, so loudly that the courtroom attendant had to knock on the window to tell him to be quiet. He then picked up his chair and moved it next to me, and with his finger in my face, shaking the finger, saying "You would not be happy if he was electrocuted and dead." He then picked up his chair and slammed it down at my feet and left the room. I was absolutely mortified at his actions, and frightened of this man who was supposed to be a professional human being, who was now throwing more than a temper fit.

All I could do was to leave the room, he holding the door as I left. He was staring at me in fury.

The advocate did nothing but stand there.

Beaufort is about a 45-minute ride from my home in Bluffton. The drive was long and waves of sickness were upon me, as I did not know how to handle this situation.

The next day I searched on the computer to find out what I could do for this type of ill treatment that I had received. I found information that I could bring charges against this person.

I wrote a letter to the proper authorities, telling them the terrible ordeal I had experienced. I also contacted the Special Prosecutor of the 14th district by sending a letter as well, and writing to the Governor of South Carolina about the horrid treatment I was given.

Here the trial was to start in two weeks, and my prosecutor made a 100% change to defend the killer of my son. I requested another prosecutor, as after the way he treated me at the bond hearing there was no way in Hell he planned on helping us get justice for Tommy. He was bent on getting the killer off.

I had not heard from the advocate after the incident with the second prosecutor. I called her and asked, "Are you being told not to talk to me?"

It was a few weeks later. She did finally call me. Her first words out of her mouth: "I am queasy."

"Why?" I asked.

"Well," she said, "I was asked to testify about the charges you told the State about the prosecutor and what went on in that room that day, and I am afraid I will lose my job."

I said, "Telling the truth about that day should not get you fired." She hung up.

These three years later, I was able to find out that she more than likely would have been fired. So does this not prove what goes on in our justice system, to be afraid to tell the truth?

Was it justice to allow a prosecutor to get away with his actions toward me? This is surely the injustice of it all, and what goes on in our so-called justice system.

I had written to Governor Nikki Haley, asking for help with my situation. I never received a reply from the Governor's office. What was in my head? Did I really think she would care? No, she did not. It was not she who lost a child to a violent act. No compassion.

I also wrote the senators, congressmen and any person I could tell the story to about my son's murder and about gun laws. Lindsay Graham was the only one to answer me, and of course he only said he believed that we have a right to arm ourselves. Okay, I thought, so I wrote back asking if he had ever had a child murdered. No reply. He could not care less either.

I contacted John McCain for help. Tommy and I both supported him, and followed him around when he visited Bluffton and Hilton Head. Never heard from him either.

I met Tom Davis, and he said he would see what he could do for me. Forget that. Also no help.

But at one point I did receive a phone call from the Davis office, as many months earlier a campaign letter came to me asking for donations. I wrote back, "Why should I help if I cannot receive help back?"

So, that caller said I could go to Columbia and speak of this story, but as a trial had not been conducted I could not speak about anything pertaining to the murder.

Around this time a wave of terrible killings in our country started the big topic of gun laws.

I had a terrible incident one evening when I attended one of the local restaurants to hear the Sheriff speak about illegal immigrants. I went, thinking I would get a chance to speak with him if he had time.

I got my dinner and sat down to eat when this guy next to me asked why I was there this night. I told him about my son being murdered and my feelings about gun laws that I felt needed to be revised. Well, did this guy go off the wall, yelling that I had no right to take away his rights to have guns, and mind you the restaurant crowd with folks for dinner and the meeting was there. Then he yelled that if I did not like what was going on, to leave the country. Short memory of this man not to realize I have rights also, but he was thinking of himself only.

Finally the second prosecutor's office called, asking me to come to his office. Still very upset from the incident with number-two prosecutor and nervous to hear what was going to take place, I was told he would have a new prosecutor from Columbia take the case.

I waited weeks, with no word from Columbia, so I made a phone call to them, only to have them tell me "We did not have your phone number." What a bunch of bull this was. I said, "You have all the paperwork there, and you could have called the Beaufort Court House. My number was sent with all the paperwork about the murder."

I then was given a name to call, only to hear this prosecutor say "Oh, I passed this case on because it is too complicated for me to do."

This is the system. Wait, and Wait. Finally I received a letter from the new advocate introducing herself, telling me about her duties to me. Basically it was the same as the other advocate did.

I did not speak with the new prosecutor for months, and finally I made a request for his attention, as this was getting ridiculous to find out what was going on.

He got around to calling me. His first statement to me was "If I do not have enough evidence I will close the case."

I remarked, "What do you mean, not enough evidence? There was enough for the first trial that was to be. So we just talked and talked back and forth and that was it. "I will be in touch again," he said.

Then the advocate's job took over. She was the correspondent with me about what was going on, and it was not much. She was very nice about everything, but it just was "wait and see" when I would hear word about any kind of trial being set.

A petition was started, and we gathered many names to be presented to the prosecutor asking that we have a trial soon. This was totally ignored, just like anything else in the Justice System, as we now have found out over the past and now going on four years, and this killer has yet to be punished.

Things are not done in this system except when they want them to be done. No compassion for families, even though we are victims wanting to see a killer behind bars.

I was asked by the advocate, "What if a jury finds this man not guilty? What are you going to do?"

My goodness, I thought. What do they expect me to do? I am not seeking revenge, as my son cannot come back to life. All I want and the family wants is justice for Tommy, as this was a senseless murder for such a horrid, evil person who tormented my son because he just wanted his garage door opener back.

The months continued and now it was more than two and a half years after the murder, and still not a mention of a trial date being set. This prosecutor never called me again.

One day in August, an unexpected phone call from the advocate came, saying that the prosecutor wanted to have a meeting with me in Bluffton at the Police Department. I was not told why, but I knew exactly what was going on, as a prosecutor would not drive from Columbia just to tell me that the case was going to trial. Earlier, when I first had the chance and the only time that I ever spoke with him, he said if he did not have enough evidence he would close the case. Well this is it, I thought.

I arrived earlier at the Police Department before the time stated for me to be there, and sat in my car, just waiting and feeling so sick and very sad, knowing that I was about to be informed that a trial would never come about.

I saw the prosecutor's car drive into the parking area, and I watched as the advocate and he got out of the car. I still was sitting for just a little longer, as my body just did not want to move.

Have to go, I said, so I opened my car door and walked toward them. The advocate said "You must be Joan." We shook hands, the normal meeting greeting.

We were ushered into this cold room. Why, I thought, does everything have to be so cold, like death?

As we sat down, the prosecutor was not sitting with us, as yet he was on the phone letting the killer's lawyer know that they had arrived to let me know of this horrid news for me, but good for the killer. The advocate talked really fast, stated the reason they were there and that it was for what I knew it to be. When the prosecutor sat down, she said to him, "I let the cat out of the bag already," as they just did not know how to go about telling me in a gentle way.

Gentle way. What? I placed my son's picture down on the table in front of them and said "This is what my son looked like," and then I presented his ashes and said "This is what I have left of him now."

The prosecutor was trying to explain things I already knew. He said he had talked with Prosecutor #2 about the "Castle Law" and said a new addition to the law had been added and it would help the killer's case. Please. Did they think I was some dummy? I knew that once a judge gave his decree of a sentence that it could not be reversed back to let a new law be accepted.

With his big law book, opened in front of him filled with sticky notes on pages he more than likely was going to talk to me about, he said a new law, called State Versus Dickey, was in play and that this would help the killer to get off. He never explained any of what it was about.

So with that it was now the end of this case, as he was going to dismiss the charges for lack of evidence. He now started to explain that if a judge had dismissed this case it could never go to a trial, as I knew that this would be called double jeopardy. So with the special prosecutor dismissing the case, it is still open and can still go to trial if evidence comes about. His statement was "a slim chance for that."

THE STATE

After the terrible incident with Prosecutor #2, I did report him to the state. I received a letter from one of the personnel that was to investigate. The heading said "Feel Free To Contact Us." Case Number: 12-DE-L0708

Sadly, my complaint against the second prosecutor was dismissed. This was my response to having found the case dismissal to be unfounded.

The advocate was in the room with me that morning. She was called to testify in this case against the second prosecutor, and she did not tell the truth, as she was afraid of losing her job.

I found this out when I received a call from the state to verbally tell me of the case being dismissed. I proceeded to go over my charges with a female official as to what happened that morning. After that conversation she said to me that what I said was not what the witness said, and I replied "Of course not" as she (the advocate) was afraid of losing her job.

I told them that they were not there, and it was I that had to endure the conduct of this man. Anyone in law enforcement must know the truth is not always told.

I proceeded to repeat the whole story of that incident once again, reminding them that the killer was a threat to Society, asking them "Where is the common sense of it all?" This second prosecutor became upset with me for asking questions. Of course he did not like this. He was taking my rights away from me.

Misconduct means "improper behavior" causing emotional distress.

This man's behavior was not only unethical and most certainly not becoming of a professional lawyer. He was hostile, and he frightened me. He caused me so much emotional distress that I ended up in the hospital.

How improper he was in all his actions, as in the way he

talked to me and the throwing down of his chair at my feet. How can anyone call this acceptable?

My word is not acceptable because a lawyer is the one protected and believed.

A lot of cronyism and favoritism goes on in the justice system. How can a common person like me be believed? I am looked down upon.

Do you think I would make a complaint knowing that it would probably hurt my son's case? I took this chance as I do not ever want to be treated like this again, and no other person should either.

The public should know of how a prosecutor can get away with this kind of misconduct that was given to me.

Where is the justice to me? There is none.

I became a victim, not only of the killer who took my son away from me, but also of the justice system itself.

THE FIFTH AMENDMENT

The Fifth Amendment was created in reaction to the excesses of the courts of Star Chamber and High Commission British courts of equity that operated from 1487-1641.

These courts utilized the inquisitorial method of truth-seeking as opposed to the prosecutorial. This meant that prosecutors did not bear the burden of proving a case, but that sufficient "proof" came from browbeating confessions out of the accused.

All this was started because in those years confessions were obtained by torture or browbeating; the amendment was based on the belief that coerced confessions were inherently unreliable, so the reason was not sufficient "proof."

These courts required the accuser to answer any questions put to him, without advance notice of his accusers, the charges against him, or evidence amassed. With the abolition of the Courts of Star Chamber and High commission, the common-law courts of England incorporated this principle of nemo tentur, that no man should be bound to accuse himself. By the 18th century, English law provided that neither confessions coerced during the trial nor pretrial confessions obtained through torture could be used.

The right to be free from self-incrimination was established in nine states and was a tenet of common law throughout most of the colonies before it appeared in the United States Constitution. Since then, the U.S. Supreme Court has expanded the Fifth Amendment to apply not only to criminal proceedings and pretrial proceedings in criminal matters, including police station interrogations, but to any other proceeding, civil or criminal, formal or informal.

The Fifth Amendment was created because the founding fathers wanted to protect rights of the accused. They objected to many of the ways they were treated by the British in matters of crime and justice. Hence, the Fifth Amendment provides for many protections from unfair methods of prosecution and investigation.

This Amendment was created when militias were not really regulated, but then it became necessary to the security of becoming a free state, which is giving the right of people to keep and bear arms. This is the Second Amendment. These were different times in our society, and these many years later the Amendments do show the unfairness in application, especially when it comes to the Fifth.

When a murder is committed and the killer admits to it on his own without being forced into saying he was involved in the crime, why should this person then have the right to invoke the Fifth Amendment *after* admitting to killing someone? Common sense must be used to bring balance to the application of the Fifth Amendment.

What right did this person have to take away the ultimate right of another human being in depriving him of his life? This law allows a killer to escape any kind of a punishment. It is not fair and this needs to be changed to account for situations in which there is no doubt of the physical fact of who killed the victim, as was the case in the murder of my son.

Because of the overly-applied Fifth Amendment, and because of a justice system which did not at least pursue the truth and present a case to a jury, I will not see a speedy and public trial because of this law.

The killer admitted that he was the shooter, and the law can protect *him*? Why? The victim is dead, and the killer can say anything to try and save himself, telling lies to protect him from the consequences which are due in cases of cold-blooded murder such as this one.

There is no actual proof that the victim was going to harm the killer. The victim was unarmed and in very poor health. Logic dictates that there should have been a trial. The entire concept of justice cries for a trial in this case.

In a particular affront to what is right, the killer now has decided to sue the Police Department for false arrest. False arrest? He killed a man. He was arrested for killing the man. He was incredibly fortunate that the state dropped the case. And so he sues the police and prosecutors for giving him a lucky break? The audacity, the insult to justice and fairness, is appalling.

So when a murder is committed and the killer confesses, and then says "Hey, I got the Fifth Amendment behind me," the killer walks free. The victim is dead and cannot plead for himself. How can this be declared as a right in the favor of a killer? He does not need to say one word, and he walks away as a free man.

ON THE SUBJECT OF DRUGS

It bothers me terribly, after reading and re-reading the police incident reports, that they assumed my son was into heavy street drugs. Tommy was on Xanax for the stress that he was experiencing. He was also dealing with Lilith and her use of the Xanax as well. Tommy realized that he was not in a good position, and as time went by he wanted to get away from Lilith and her intent to continue using Tommy's Xanax. But she would not leave him alone.

It is important to point out that the medication bottles found by the police were prescribed to Tommy by a doctor for the pain he had in his back, as he was in constant pain. He had pain medicines injected into his back every three months.

I drove Tommy to Charleston in July of 2010 for his fiftieth birthday, where the doctor performed surgery on his back. For two weeks, he had not been able to walk. He was in such a bad condition that he was told not to use stairs anymore, whether up or down. He was on multiple pills for his pain. Hence, it is frustrating that all the police did was see the prescription drugs at his home and make the assumption, very unfairly, that he was somehow an abuser of drugs. Doctors are not in the habit of prescribing drugs to people who don't need them. Tommy needed them.

None of us, as parents, ever wants our children to be involved in drugs, or to involve themselves with people who want drugs for recreation or to sell or share. I wish that Tommy had never met Lilith, as he is dead because he got involved with the wrong person. I am sad to know that he realized before his death that it was a mistake to allow her into his life and his home and to have access to his drugs. I do not make excuses for Tommy's poor judgment in letting Lilith use and either share or sell his drugs. But he most certainly did not deserve to die as a result of poor judgment. He simply wanted his garage door opener back, and to discontinue an ill-advised friendship with this woman. And the murderer is free to do it again, perhaps to the next man Lilith becomes entangled with.

THE GALL OF IT ALL

Mind you now, the killer has now decided to sue the Bluffton Police Department, alleging that he was falsely accused. They just did their job, that evening and in the ensuing investigation.

According to all police reports and all information available, the investigation was done according to all laws and regulations for police work. The killer CONFESSED that evening that he was the shooter of my son. The police found his gun on the trunk of his car. Naturally the investigation would have to be geared toward determining whether the killer shot my son in cold blood, or whether the shooting was necessary in any way. If it was not necessary, then charges of either murder or manslaughter would have to be pursued. In pursuing charges, the police department did what they are supposed to do: in the absence of a good and reasonable self-defense motive, the killer would have to be charged with a punishable homicide. In no way should the state's failure to bring the case to trial be any reflection on the Bluffton Police Department's intentions or integrity in investigating homicides and properly accusing admitted shooters of intentional homicide.

The killer is free today because he invoked the Fifth Amendment and because his girlfriend lied to protect him from the consequences that are supposed to come with murdering people. It is not the Bluffton Police Department's fault that Wayne killed Tommy Mullins. And it is not Tommy Mullins's fault that Wayne killed him. It is Wayne's own fault. The police simply did their jobs appropriately and fairly. When the state prosecution did not do their jobs in pursuing justice, a killer walked free. He should be enormously relieved, thanking the devil for his luck, for surely God would not set this man free. To sue the police department for doing their jobs is an insulting slap in the face to all citizens who believe in justice and fairness in society.

I also heard it mentioned that the situation leading to my son's murder was an "ongoing dispute." How can you call this a dispute when all Tommy wanted was his right to have his garage door opener given back to him?

The killer and his girlfriend refused to give it back. This was no "dispute," but rather a refusal to return someone else's property. Tommy was not being aggressive and threatening toward the killer that evening. In the first place, the killer left the inside of his home and sneaked out of his garage. Why did the killer not call the police? The reason is that he actually wanted Tommy dead. The girlfriend said in the police interview that Tommy took one step. Mind you, one step...and he was killed from a distance of thirteen feet. One step by a disabled man is hardly "aggressive and threatening."

The killer has now taken this to the federal courts, claiming abuse of process, negligence and even conspiracy by the police. This is crazy. Does the killer think for one second that the Bluffton police made up a story, when the killer himself admitted to shooting my son? Is this not insane?

Why should this killer be protected? First, there was never any proof that Tommy ever tried to break into their home. Second, Tommy was unarmed. Third, he was ambushed, despite being unarmed and disabled. Here we have two killers, one who shot a man dead for wanting his garage door opener back, and then took the Fifth Amendment to avoid incriminating himself, and one who made it happen, and then took the Fifth Amendment in order to avoid incriminating herself. She even participated in the murder by watching her boyfriend get his gun and sneak out to kill Tommy, all the while doing nothing to discourage her boyfriend from doing so.

They want the blame to be on Tommy for his own death. They do not want to accept responsibility for the terrible crime they committed. They are cowards, and much below that.

This was a senseless killing that could have been avoided, but Lilith just would not leave Tommy alone, because he had told her that he did not want to be friends with her anymore, which she could not accept, as proven by her texts to Tommy.

The killer did not have a trial only because of lies, as the dead person could not defend himself or be there to speak the truth. Lies were told by the killer and his girlfriend to protect themselves. The killer has taken advantage of the justice system by pleading the Fifth, and the girlfriend has avoided testifying against the killer by also pleading the Fifth. What does this say about them? "I will not incriminate myself. I am guilty and do not want to go to prison." That is what this says about them. Two people committed a horrendous crime. They agreed to lie about what happened, and then pleaded the Fifth in order to avoid hard questioning aimed at the truth. To think that just one law or amendment can protect killers is beyond comprehension.

The killer now says "Oh poor me" in his effort to sue the justice system. He is not accepting that he is a murderer, and that the police were doing their jobs when they arrested him after he admitted that he killed an unarmed, disabled man.

The killer's defense lawyer received big bucks from Lilith's parents to somehow avoid a long prison sentence for Lilith's boyfriend. How low can one get? I wonder how lawyers like this one can live with themselves for defending cold-blooded killers. It must be the money. Yes, it must be the big bucks. There certainly is no compassion from such a man for the innocent. He helped a killer go free, and he walked away saying he did a great job. Is this not sickening?

The life of a good man was taken away from me, and from his daughter, and from our entire family.

TRIBUTES AND REMINISCENCES

In remembrance of Tommy Mullins, here are the words of family and friends:

"I was young when I knew Tommy Mullins. He had a booming voice, animated personality and it was obvious that he lived out loud! Simply put, he was full of life. And even though he lived life with this loud enthusiasm, you could tell he was passionate and committed to his family and friends."

"I knew Tommy Mullins because our fathers were good friends. In fact, I call Tommy's parents 'Aunt' and 'Uncle.' I remember as a kid Tommy was fun to be around, even though he was a little older than me. Whether swimming at the county park or at 'family' gatherings, like Thanksgiving dinner, I enjoyed hanging out and talking to him. He always seemed to live and enjoy life to the fullest."

"My name is Patricia Mullins Ametrano and I am the victim's sister. I would like everyone to know about my brother. He was a man of great strength and loved his family so very much. He was always there for us. His laughter was heartfelt and very contagious. He was there for my mother when we lost our father. He was not only a brother but a father; he was not just a son, but was a good friend to many. He was an uncle who was loved by his nieces and nephews. He was a person; a person who deserved to live. I just wish that he was not taken from me because I had so much to say to him and never had the opportunity. I miss him and deeply wish I had the chance to make things better between us, but that chance was taken from me. I just hope in his heart he knows that I always loved him...

It's hard to lose a family member in general, but to have a life taken at the hands of another person is not something anyone should have to read. Tommy, you are missed and loved..."

"A Toast to Tommy...His beautiful smile, his laugh, both were very contagious when you were with him. He was one of a kind...very loving, a great listener, and a good brother and special friend to me. And oh yes, he was a Poet. I dearly miss him and when I get sad missing him, I think of the times we spent together during his life that consisted of fun...sad... happy...good and challenging times. He was there for all that needed him, and he would be the first to give you his last dollar or the shirt off his back if you needed it. My baby brother and I have so many memories that are very close to my heart and will forever be cherished. His life came to an end on Friday, 11/19/2010 by another man's hand!
I love you, Tommy and miss you so much!

Your sister, Donna

TOMMY'S KINDNESS TO A HANDICAPPED NEIGHBOR

Tommy used to live in a small apartment complex. This nice lady who had physical handicaps lived a few doors down from Tommy. They became friends, and Tommy would take her to church or to the store. She had to use a wheelchair, and Tommy would help her in and out of this big unstable chair. It was so hard for her to maneuver and to get around. Tommy was always ready to help her.

Tommy was instrumental in getting the apartment complex to build a wheelchair ramp near her apartment. This made her life better, as she was now able to get to her car without help. The woman wanted to thank Tommy for his kindness, so she bought him a Bible, inscribed with his childhood nickname. Needless to say, Tommy cherished this gift, which was inscribed on the cover: **Tom (Moon) Mullins**

NOVEMBER 23, 1994

Tommy wrote the following poem after the death of a loved one. He was a very compassionate man.

On a cold November morning, Sadness crept our way,
The news, we've lost a loved one, has stilled our hearts.
Today
And the future holds the pain we'll save for all the coming
years, of the memories and the laughter, the pain, and all
the tears
We bid farewell to you today, and may God rest your
Soul
You're in our hearts forever more and your love will always
Hold.

Good-bye.....Marion

CHEESECAKE

Tommy and his daughter Katie attended Sunday church. This particular day, he was to bring a dish to share with the congregation.

Tommy's love of this cheesecake recipe, one that he had baked before and shared, made him want to bring cheesecake to the church event. He mixed cottage cheese, sour cream, cream cheese, sugar, and all the other ingredients that were needed for this cake. Greasing the spring form pan, then filling it, was easy. Tommy plopped it into the oven, which had achieved the correct temperature. The directions called for baking for one hour, then turning the oven off and letting the cheesecake sit for another hour to settle.

Well, to his surprise, Tommy's cheesecake did not bake the way it usually did, so after discovering the disaster, he had no idea what to do. Then an idea hit him, and he shared it with me: he would just put it into a large bowl and take it to church as a pudding.

Everybody loved Tommy's pudding, and it was eaten by all. My son was an inventive soul!

FISH TANKS

Tommy's interest in tank fish became far more than he realized. He decided to make a different kind of fish tank in hopes of marketing them..

The assembly, the putting together of an unique fish tank from his own idea proved a little more challenging than he expected, but with determination he gathered the materials and his design, and he made it, one he called a better leak-free tank than ones which were factory made. It was well built. He showed me how he finished the sides and bottom, which were different in his concept for being leak-proof. However, the financial cost of making his tank was more than he expected for marketing it.

To my surprise, Tommy gave it to me. Tommy already had a very large aquarium with his odd-looking fish, the kind where one would not dare to put one's hand in the water or you would find a fish hanging from it.

Tommy launched me on a new adventure. Taking me to the pet shop, he described all these little fish that would be just right for this new and different kind of aquatic home.

Before I could buy the ones I liked, he pointed out that I had to make sure I had the correct ingredients for water PH, temperature, and all the things that were needed to make the water compatible for the fish. Tommy also explained about the pump, and all that was needed to keep the water churning. The little plants were also important for keeping the water maintained with a certain amount of oxygen, and to provide resting and hiding places for all the newcomers to my home.

So off to my home we went.

Tommy filled the tank with water and completed putting all the ingredients into it. He showed me how I had to take daily water samples to make sure the water stayed at the correct pH levels. By the next day we would be able to go back to the pet shop, as twenty-four hours of the water getting to the right temperature had to be accomplished, in addition to producing the correct pH, for the survival of these little creatures.

I wanted Tommy to help me pick out different species and colors, as I knew nothing about the care of fish. But of course I bought a book to follow instructions for their care.

The tank was a nice size, and Tommy cautioned me about buying different species so they would be compatible for living with each other. He also advised me not to buy more than a certain amount. So with his guidance I bought about ten little creatures. They were so adorable. With anticipation we drove home quickly, as we did not want the fish harmed from insufficient oxygen, as without it they would die before they got into their new home.

Net in hand, Tommy carefully transferred each fish from box to tank. We watched them swim around in their vast new home.

This was a challenging venture for me. It was time-consuming and worrisome, as these creatures were so helpless without my care. Even though I followed Tommy's directions, time would show that these little creatures could become sick. When they did, the water had to be treated so that others would not become ill.

A male and female of a particular species became the fun couple to watch. They were always together, and their resting place was this one corner of the tank. They were never without each other.

The tank had to be kept cleaned. I faithfully made sure that it was. One day, I cleaned the tank and replenished all that it needed, checking to make sure I completed it correctly. I went about my day. Later this day, as my husband and I were sitting at the table for dinner, you could see the tank clearly, as I kept it in a special spot in my kitchen because we enjoyed watching the fish playing. After a little while, my husband said, "Where is the fish that's always in the corner?"

I jumped up. "No!" I cried as I ran to the tank. I looked all over, and could not see this fish in the tank. I had cleaned the tank that day, and could not imagine where it had gone. I then thought to move the tank away from the wall, and there it was.

I did not know that fish could jump. All I could imagine was that when I had the top off the tank, he must have jumped up and fell out onto the counter behind the tank. I was devastated, and cried. I felt terrible, as I had not been attentive enough that something like this could happen.

The very sad, sad ending to this is that the mate of this fish never left the corner of the tank again. Within a week, it had passed away. Yes, I learned that a fish can die of a broken heart.

I hated to tell Tommy, as he was a passionate person and I knew he would feel this loss as well.

This story will always be a memorable one for me, as lessons are learned about Love, Life and Death. We as humans feel Love, and God did create even a fish to feel Love.

A NIGHT AT "THE NUTCRACKER"

I asked Tommy if he would want to join me to see the ballet, *The Nutcracker*, a ballet that has been around for years and is presented and performed around the holidays every year. Tommy had already met the couple who presented my ballet story on stage, and they were putting on this production of the holiday classic. He said yes, that he wanted to go, and during this beautiful presentation I looked over to see Tommy crying. I asked him what was wrong.

"Nothing," Tommy said. "It's just that I did not realize how beautiful the ballet was." He was very emotional about this.

My son appreciated beauty in all its forms, and wasn't afraid to express himself emotionally. That was one of the beautiful things about him.

A GRUFF VOICE AND A GENTLE SOUL

Tommy had a gruff voice, so many people thought he was a tough guy, when indeed his heart was soft. I remember Tommy talking loudly, not long after he moved into his Bluffton home and was meeting people. One guy said, "You're okay. I like you. You are not the way you sound."

It bothered Tommy that people sometimes thought from his gruff voice that he might not be a nice person, when he absolutely was. But as people in Bluffton began to know him, they could see that he really was a good guy.

Tommy was a gentle man. I remember him coming to me one day with a wolf spider in his hand, to show me how big this spider was. I had never seen this kind of spider before, but somehow it got into his home. The spider was startlingly large, with this black body and large hairy legs. Tommy had the creature in its temporary home of a plastic bag with punched holes for air.

I had never seen this particular species before. Rocky had spotted it, and even at a hundred pounds he backed off when it was crawling around. But Rocky, brave Rocky, with his front paws in a down position scratching the floor, started to approach the spider as dogs do. This hairy spider with legs crawling toward Rocky made it look like this was going to be a big confrontation. Well, Tommy of course grabbed this spider before either one of them got close enough for the battle. So this amusing story does end happily, as far as we know.

After showing me the wolf spider, Tommy released this hairy creature to its freedom in my yard, and off it went. He just could not kill it. That's the way he was.

AN EXAMPLE OF A GOOD SON

I often said to myself, "Thank goodness for Tommy," as he was always there for me, changing my light bulbs and doing simple jobs that had to be done, especially ones which he was able to handle even with his bad back.

One job in particular was when I wanted to get a new screen front door for my home. The old one I referred to as my "ole" country door, because when it shut it banged like an old farm door. I could not just get rid of it, for sentimental reasons, so I needed a new screen door for the front, and for the "ole" country door to go into another spot I had picked out. I used a handyman to install the new door, and explained where the old door was to go. The handyman grumbled to find a way to install it, as it needed some adjustments to fit where I wanted it, but finally he got it installed. I thought, "Great!"

After the guy left, Tommy arrived and opened the door to take a look at it. He said, "Mom, look what this guy did." I looked. To my shock, he had taken the existing panel and cut it all apart, as he did not know how to attach the hook and screw.

"Not to worry, Mom!" Tommy said. "I will fix it."

Tommy went and bought the wood filler and started the repair. He did a little at a time every day, because the previous fill needed time to dry. We took a picture of it, because we could not believe something so simple as to attach a hook and screw became this "screwed-up job."

As days passed, all was repaired. Tommy then sanded the door down and painted the panel. You could never tell where the damage was, as he had done such a wonderful repair job. And of course, the bang is just what I wanted. Like having a country door on a porch.

That's what Tommy was like. He wanted to give back himself

to people. He loved the Bible, and at one point I was encouraging him to become a pastor. He felt that he was not good enough. He taught me a lot about the Bible, and we had many discussions. Especially about Revelations.

TOMMY, THE BIBLE AND ME

Tommy and I had many conversations about the Bible. One chapter we discussed often was Revelations. He would read to me different happenings to come at the end of all life, and we would have our discussions and thoughts given to each other.

The other day I bought a small hand Bible with larger than usual print for my everyday reading of the Bible. I have read Revelations before at random, but it seemed this day it became a positive sign for me to read.

I believe in unusual happenings, so when I opened to Revelations, Chapter 21, without looking for this page, my eyes automatically fixed on Verse 8.

I know in some way that discovering this passage was for the purpose of helping me get through the lack of justice in seeing the killer walk free. As follows, here is the passage:

But the fearful, and unbelieving, and the abominable,and the murderers, and the whoremongers, and sorcerers, and the idolaters, and all the liars, shall have their part in the lake which burneth with fire and brimstone which is the second death.

I have to believe both the killer and his girlfriend will be sentenced to this second death, a punishment for the senseless killing of Tommy.

ROCKY'S FATE

Tommy loved his dog Rocky. He exclaimed many times that Rocky saved his life. Tommy would tell me that when he was down and under, having Rocky to care for kept him going, as did the great love Rocky had for Tommy.

After the murder, my grandson, also named Tommy, offered to care for Rocky, saying he would take him back to live with him. Unfortunately, this would not be a happy ending for Rocky. The apartment complex where my grandson lived did not allow dogs over fifty pounds to live there. Rocky was all of a hundred pounds. My grandson told the landlords the story of his uncle being murdered, but rules are rules, and they said they could not break them.

With sadness, Grandson Tommy had to find a new home for Rocky. Finding a man who raised boxers, Tommy told the story of his uncle's death, so with yet more sadness Rocky was taken to his new home.

Rocky had health issues; he was seven years old when Tommy was murdered. It is now several years since Rocky had to go to a new home. More than likely, Rocky has passed and is now with his beloved owner.

A MOTHER'S DAY LETTER

On May 9th, 1982, I received this Mother's Day letter from Tommy. Any mother would cherish a letter such as this one:

Dear Mom,

Well, it's Mother's Day again, and you're there and I'm here...but my words can't tell you how wonderful and great you have always been to all us kids. You deserve today, and 364 days more of Mother's Days. Now that you're "away" so to speak, I realize how important a role you played in my life, always there when I needed you (and at more times), always loving us, and caring for us even if our morals were different. You stayed with us and never let us go—and to me that is what mothering is all about. I love you forever—

Have a Happy Mother's Day, and even if it's raining, I know the sun will be shining only on you, Mom. I hope to see you soon. Very soon. So take care—always thinking of you—

Love you,

Tom

ONE BIRTHDAY AND CHRISTMAS

It was the early morning of my birthday, and Tommy came bounding into the house with flowers and a card saying "Happy Birthday Mom!"

"The flowers are beautiful, Tommy," I said to him.

Smiling, he said, "Wait a minute, I forgot something!" He ran out of the house and returned with a new computer monitor, remarking "Mom, you need a new one," and quickly seeing if it was the size to fit on the stand. He said, "Oh please let it be the right size!" and it was. Tommy felt that the other one I had was so old that he just wanted me to have an updated one. His heart was always caring.

Now for Christmas he gave me my card and beautiful flowers, as he always did. But this day he also said "I have something else for you!" as he dashed out the door. In a few minutes he came back in with a new TV. "Well Mom, it is about time you have a new TV," and he was right, as the other one I had was over fifteen years old. "I hope this fits," he said, beaming, and he hooked it up to the wires. But the TV was not tall enough to reach eye level, so he ran out of the house, saying he would be right back. In a little while he returned with a small drawer. He put the TV on it, and it lifted it up to just the right line of sight.

How many special memories I have of my dear Son. He truly was thinking of my happiness.

A LETTER AND POETRY FROM DAUGHTER KATIE

Dear Father, Daddy;

Dear Tommy, Family;

Dear "Moon", Friends;

Dear Tom, Acquaintances;

Dear Audience, Unknown;

This letter is neither relevant nor irrelevant. It (simply) is a compilation of thoughts and memories for all, dedicated to my father, Thomas Leonard Mullins Jr. (11 July 1960 - 19 November 2010).

One week (prior to) before your passing I received the last e-mail you'd have the opportunity to send. Within it were your words to never forget the truth behind the meaning of this music: ("Time" by Pink Floyd).

Speaking of Pink Floyd, I did have the opportunity to see Roger Waters perform "The Wall" live. It was the most intense experience to witness the works of brilliant musicians with superb choreography. During the first ten minutes I bawled with the ecstasy of excitement and appreciation for this rare opportunity, understanding that before long, within my lifetime, there will never be another chance. Behind these emotions was nostalgia, a creeping sadness that my father couldn't have joined me, and the realization that I would never be able to tell him about this moment. He would never know, he would never feel the joy that sharing this experience would bring.

This reminds me of the time I unexpectedly saw Kansas at Fall for Greenville in 2007. The moment I realized it wasn't a cover band I called my dad. He couldn't understand a word I was saying so I called him later that night.

Music. It's something we always had in common. A shared love of classic rock. Even if I did listen to mainstream pop as a young girl, I was raised on good old classic rock. He certainly influenced (shaped) my musical tastes.

Happy times still come at a cost. The price of pain because you cannot, nor ever have the ability, to share your life's memories. Each one is special and important. That's what makes time so precious, delicate. It's not a secret: it is terribly limited. As long as you are enjoying your time, it cannot be wasted. Regardless of how microscopic our lifetime is on a grand scale, it is the luxury of existence that must be cherished as long as we are conscious beings.

There are many (moments/times) where I sit on the verge of tears, lingering in the (emotion - word I could not think of at the time - shadows...) of remembrance and longing. I long for those bear hugs you gave every time you saw me. I only had the chance once, maybe twice, not to utter, "It's too tight!" I finally understood what it is to be filled with so much love that when you know you are lucky enough, in enough good health, to be with the people you love, that you want to hold on tight and never let go. It's an understanding of how limited time really is.

He loved fish tanks, and he was especially fond of Oscars. We always had good memories of setting up tanks and caring for our pets. It was always emotional when we lost one.

My father, he always was a sensitive man. In tune with his emotions enough to let them take hold. I've heard him grieve, I've heard him mourn. When loved ones were lost I would be there to wrap my arms around him and comfort him. He felt pain, he felt sadness. He was human.

He felt joy and happiness. When he watched the Giants games and would rave by the television. When we went out and explored cities. We have kayaked, gone horseback riding, visited museums, gone on school field trips, visited the beach and their shops, amusement parks, gone out for dinner and ice cream, completed school projects, taken care of each other when sick, played board games and card games (competitively even), wrote, gone for walks, played putt-putt, took minor road trips. We have had to break into our house when a key was lost, argued, cried, laughed. He was my daddy and always will be.

Michael and Thomas, I know he always loved and missed you two terribly. He was very open-minded toward your feelings and beliefs. I know that, more than anything, he longed to see us happy, even to be reunited one day.

My father wanted more than anything to bring joy into people's hearts, strangers or not. He would flatter people, tell jokes and make humorous (even smart-aleck - I get this from him) remarks. He would cook and bake. I have many fond memories of cooking various (mainly Italian) dishes and baking, namely our family recipe cheesecake (it is fantastic—unique flavor and texture that you cannot find anywhere else).

He was very active in the church community. When he was healthy enough to, he would play the drums (which was one of his favorite pastimes). He cooked a nice meal and brought it to a family in need. This particular church was part of a program where needy families are able to travel between various churches for shelter for a limited amount of time. We spoke with the adults and played with the children.

Now I would like to take some time to discuss the dark injustice brought upon my father. He would never be around to see me graduate. He will never see his children grow up, accomplish their life goals, get married, and he will never meet his grandchildren.

Foremost, I would like to mention the poor health of my father. He had severe degenerative osteo-arthritis for years, as far back as I can remember. This condition mainly affected his hips and back. Around 2008 he had been diagnosed with a newly discovered (in the medical community) birth defect in his hip. He was diagnosed with sleep apnea and required an oxygen tank. In 2009 he had surgery, and in 2010 they discovered complications with that surgery so he would have to undergo further surgical procedures to correct those, and more for his back. He had high risk for cancer of the esophagus. He had an enlarged liver, and issues with his kidneys and stomach. Essentially the healthiest part of his body was his heart.

His most recent surgery was in July of 2010, just four months before he was shot in the chest and murdered. He was recovering, taking medications; practically in poor enough shape to be harmless. He was supposed to be walking with the aid of a walker. As a matter of fact, that is the only reason he had to communicate with his neighbors, and that is the sole reason for their communication. They were acting as caretakers for our beloved dog, Rocky.

As previously mentioned, my father was an emotional person. Like any other human, he has gotten upset and said some things he never truly meant. He was always apologetic, and always hurt by the idea of hurting others. However, I know that in the event my father is upset enough to yell, he would be loud enough for the neighbors to be alerted. He lived in a town home, every home being too-close-for-comfort, with two homes per house. Had this ravaging emotional state, as described by the person who committed this heinous crime, occurred, at least two of the four households within that vocal range would have noticed. Due to the curvature of the community there would have been an echo that may have alarmed other households a distance away. Why, then, was there no sign of a disturbance/ no sign of danger before the gunshot? How could it be that with the message recording my grandmother wrote about, he would go from merely pleading to forcefully demanding? The real question here might be: How the Hell did he manage to lunge forward for an attack? Perhaps he lost his balance and was falling forward. He was helpless, and the killer took advantage of that state, and for what? It was senseless. Unlike him, this family at least has their morals intact.

FATHER

Son, Father, Brother, Uncle, Friend,
Tonight you've endured
Two years of rest.
Be aware of Time you cannot take back,
Knowing there will never be another
Opportunity.
Do not take Today for granted,
For Tomorrow is not guaranteed.
Moment of Remembrance,
Remind me why I strive,
Why life will not skip a beat,
Why time isn't going anywhere.
Pointless. There is no "Why"
When a thief Steals
That which cannot be
Returned.
Justice lives in our Hearts.

19 November 2012

THE GREAT EQUALIZER

The sky paints a reminiscent sight,
Blackbirds fly freely through the sky,
Massive clouds glow in the night.
You speak to me through the moon and the stars
Your memory revived in the blood-red sunset.
I wish you could witness such beauty,
But where you are in peace
surpasses all the wonders of the world.
These visions haunt me, of your body
helpless in a pool of blood.
Undeserving of sick passion,
you were left for dead.
Your vague memory leaves a legacy in the air;
each storm that passes,
each worthy lyric heard.
Guilt treads within me
for two years passed since I had seen you living.
I'm here to visit, daddy,
but it is a vacant body I am here to see.
No more laughter
no more pain.
Unbelievable tragedy,
a family torn apart, reunited in death.
You left me with a great impression
for your words always lent to me a good lesson.
But I never admitted.
You taught me kindness;
In your lesson to never be fearful of the self,
I learned appreciation for every being.
You taught me in your passing, as well.
You taught me to love
and to never hold out on the promise of tomorrow.

It is in this great unity
you've enhanced my perception:
to look into the eyes of the living
and see only death.
It is this unity in the great divider
that allows a painful love into my heart.
Acceptance is simple,
but I will never forget.
Life is only a passing entity.
We are a generation,
as were the living a thousand years before.
Allow the moment to penetrate into your being;
Time won't stop for anyone.

2 December 2010

A PRAYER SHAWL

Sometimes kindness arrives in the wake of tragedy. This happened for me when I was having to take care of all the funeral arrangements, which are still a blur to me.

A friend of mine gave me a "prayer shawl" on the day of Tommy's funeral. I had never heard of a prayer shawl before, but when I wore it, right away I felt the comfort given to me by this wonderful, person.

When I was burying my son, standing by his grave, an attendant from the church gave me another prayer shawl, saying "I believe you can use this shawl." As I put it around me, I received this enormous feeling of warmth, especially on one of my shoulders. I know this was God's hand upon me, to let me know he was with me at this terrible time in my life. What a sustaining moment it was.

I keep the shawls on the back of my chair, using them when needed. The embrace of comfort and care can still be felt. I want to thank all the caring people who take time to knit these special shawls, and the people who care to give one to a person in need. They truly are a comfort. Both of these shawls, one a gift from a friend, and one a gift from the church, serve to show me that when people work in partnership with God, comfort and peace move within reach. I may not always be able to find them, but thanks to the love of God and the kindness of friends, I do find comfort and peace often enough to feel right, rather than feel vengeful, in pursuing justice for my son.

THE FLAG

Tommy's neighbor was employed by the government to repair airplanes overseas. A long-time custom is to fly the American flag over the base in honor of a friend or family member.

Tommy's friend did this, and surprised him with the American flag and certificate saying they flew the American flag over the base to honor Tommy. This was in June of 2010.

Tommy felt so honored that a friend had done this for him.

When Tommy did not fly the flag outside of his house, his friend asked why, as this was what one was to do, but Tommy said he so appreciated this honor that he did not want the outside elements to destroy the flag. He kept it in his cabinet, where he could appreciate the honor that was given to him and for him to see every day.

This was really an honor for Tommy, as he was murdered five months later.

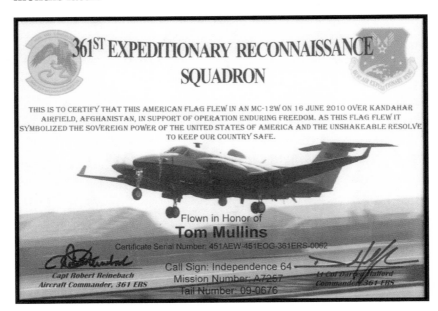

POETRY TIMES

MULLINS, THOMAS LEONARD JR. Born: New Jersey, July 11, 1960; Poems: 'I Wonder,' 1984 *American Poetry Anthology*; Themes: Mostly of life and its meaning, how life treats you and how I should treat life. (I write) to relive one's anxiety and to forward my outlook to the future. (I try to express) the reality of life around us. Hopefully my poems my poems will express feelings upon other people to let them think about the reality of life itself and what it holds.

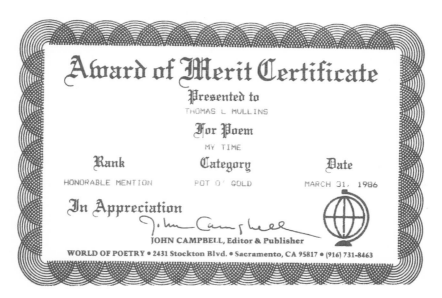

THE POETRY OF TOMMY MULLINS

TIME

Time, an endurance for all—
Something we all take for granted
As we let it slip by—
Something so special
We forget it's there.

The most respected, influenced
Need of all—
The soul verse of Life...Time

Something we need—
But never believe in (as of yet)
But as Time goes on you'll find...
It's too late...

Joan C. Mullins

THE DREAM (THAT NEVER WAS)

As I walked along the golden shores
Of a land so far away,
I fell into a distant dream,
I only wish could stay...

But then I noticed something strange,
As I looked up to the sky,
A light had shed a tear on me,
As I drew a heavy sigh

I walked along a little while,
The waves crashed against the sand,
I realize now the dream I'm in
Is not a distant land...

I stopped to climb a grassy dune,
To look atop its peak,
To have life's questions fall in hand,
And the answers people seek...

How sad the world be,
These times it's terror,
The weapons, the power, the strength,
Is no error...

To have all answers by my side,
To me would be all wrong,
For they could not solve all Man's mistakes,
They built up far too long...

I opened up my eyes
To find a dream that never was.
It's reality that's out there now,
A war of push and shove...

I WONDER

Sometimes I wonder
Just how my life should be,
The world is seen through different eyes,
And they seek to find the key.
And I wonder if I'll ever be the runner
Of my dreams
And keep my life's reality,
Though impossible it seems.

And I wonder if I'll struggle
Through the wars of poverty,
And keep my head above the grade
And the waste below my knees.
I guess we all have to wonder
About the future and its holds,
So catch your dreams before they die,
And keep them from turning cold...

Joan C. Mullins

POINT OF VIEW

The night is calm,
The air is still
As emotions fill up my mind,
I look to see what my future holds
A key, I no longer can find.

I close my eyes,
As if to be granted a wish,
And hope for a dream come true.
But this envision I hold is really a dream,
And is something I have to do.

You see, "Life is what you make it,"
A saying that holds true.
But sometimes it takes some (people) longer
To make this their point of view...

STARTING OVER

I was standing out on
The ridges—as I stared
Into the sky, my past
Just swept before me—
As I hung my head to cry...

When I looked on down
Below me—I saw a given
Light, my past was now
My future...Now I've got
To stay and fight.

Starting over, I know
it's not easy to do. But it's
Time now, to take a stand
And change your bad to good.

Starting over—"The world is
just a stage." There's something in
the words he wrote,
that broke his lifeless cage.

THE LONELY MAN

As he stands alone, and views an open sea...you can
read the pain on his face, or you can't see...
He's the lonely man—and he sings his lonely song—
With an open mind...he can't be right, he can't be wrong.

Down by the high tide line, he walks the golden sands,
Dragging all his memories, of his search to find his land.
Gazing out along the shores—his past runs hand and hand—
Now his dreams are his future dreams; it's a cost, but it's
the plan.

He's the lonely man—as he falls down to his knees, and
cries aloud,
Lord, oh can't you see—I've found the door after ninety
lonely years—tell me where's the key—
to my youth-filled days and tears.

Joan C. Mullins

I CAN SEE NOW

I can see now, we're
The players of this land—
Acting out society, as we
Prey on open hands—

THE ONES WHO DON'T BELIEVE

It may come that those—
The ones who don't believe—
The stories that they give
Are nightmares, no dreams, reality...

MY TIME

As I lay there looking down at myself,
I begin to see the light. It draws closer and closer and
                              Then!!!
Almost without a sound, the light speaks.
I hear the low tone voice, but not with my ears...
I just hear it.
                              Strange...

Then I see my loved ones, but wait!!!
I have not seen them for years...at least,
That is, I cannot remember...
                              Strange...

It's almost like I'm floating. Suspended in space, I
I drift and drift. I feel at such speed...Why?
                              Strange...

My mind I can think so crystal clear,
No error...
No twice thinking,
I speak without talking,
Hear without listening,
See, without looking...

God, is it really my time?

MY METAMORPHOSIS

Soon after the murder of my son, I wrote the following:

Like a butterfly, I am Pupa.

The ringing doorbell awakened me. Sleepily, I turned over to see what time the clock was announcing. It was eleven fifteen! I thought, Oh, what an odd time of night for anyone to visit.

As I put on my bathrobe and went to the door, I peeked out the window to see two men standing there, wearing official police badges. Opening the door, they asked my name.

"Yes, I am this person."

"We're sorry to inform you, but your son has had an accident."

"Oh, no!" I cried out. "Was he driving his car?"

"No," they answered. He was shot and killed by one of his neighbors."

I remember sitting down and the police asking questions, and my answering, but I did not know what I was answering. The police said I should have a friend stay overnight with me. I called my friend and my brother. They both came over, but the night was a blur. I never went to sleep.

The next day, I had to make arrangements for my son's funeral. I wanted to have him cremated, and to lay him next to his dad at the columbarium. First, I needed family to arrive for the viewing. That day was filled with enormous sadness, to see my son lying there and not moving. I touched him and kissed his forehead, as if he might just get up and say "Hi."

A few days later, I laid him to rest and had one of his original poems put in with his ashes. I think he knew what really happened to him, because his poem was called "My Time." He saw his own death!

Realizing that a terrible hand of one human being took another's life was unthinkable! The following days, I did not know how to react; cry? Scream? I don't even remember what I did. Within an instant my son was permanently gone from his and my human life. No more eight a.m. calls that he made to me every morning. No calls during the day. No more doors opening with a yell, "Hey Mom! Where are you?" No more going for pizzas (our usual once-a-month lunch was to find out the best-tasting pizza around!). And his thoughtful bouquet of flowers he presented lovingly every month.

Where was I to be in my life? Was I to become a pupa? Everything became strange and unreal. How was I to fight reality? How was I to understand my feelings, my emotions? At times I feel comatose to confront the truth about what happened.

My emotional life is isolated somewhere in that pupa. Will I ever emerge? Yes! This I believe, just as a butterfly goes through its transformation, I will also, struggling for the acceptance of my son's death.

A THOUGHT FROM A GRIEVING MOTHER

My son Tommy was a wonderful man. Mothers do say this about any of their children, but he *really* was. His heart was always in the right place. He was so loving and caring. What more can a mom ask for?

Sadly, Tommy had his dark days, as we all have had. Finding yourself can be hard, and Tommy did go through this challenging journey, only to emerge still this loving person who would try to help others. He never lost faith in the Lord.

Tommy was remarkably excited that he would be playing drums for the church he had just become a member of: First Baptist of Bluffton. He was eagerly anticipating his musical debut when, sadly, he was murdered less than a week before he provided his first rhythm and beat.

THE ENDING

My Dear Son Tommy:

It is now going on four years that you were murdered by two evil people. Our Justice System has let you down.

Excuses are still being said. "We do not have enough evidence," but there is evidence.

They used an existing law called the State v Dickey as a guide to how not to pursue a trial. If one reads this, you will see that this law does not pertain to your murder. It is with entirely different circumstances, and it seems that with fear the prosecutors decided not to move on with a trial. Why? Did they not want to take a challenge to task? Here they are supposed to be lawyers, ones who are to help the victims, not to side with the killer. In hindsight, they have done just that.

What a travesty of our democracy, that we now have become a shaken people who can no longer believe in our justice system.

So without a trial for these two people, our God, Lord Jesus Christ, will determine their futures. Their fate is that they will end up in the lowest bowels of hell for the terrible crime they have committed against you, Tommy. And it will be for an eternity that they will suffer.

How much I love you and miss you. One day I will be able to see you again.

A LETTER TO SENATOR LINDSEY GRAHAM

March 7, 2011

Dear Mr. Graham.

This is in regards to your letter to my concerns of gun control.

For our freedoms of speech, which Thank God we still have at this time, I do appreciate your thoughts of the right to possess firearms.

If you will think out of the box for a minute, law-abiding citizens all think they have a right to possess a gun, until just one of them commits murder. Now they are not considered in my mind as a law-abiding citizen. So who can pick a law-abiding citizen ahead of time? Can you?

A guy who said he was a law-abiding citizen was a service man who thought he had a right to kill. But he murdered my SON this past November 2010.

I am so distraught as this man is out on bail and was ordered to live right down my street in his girlfriend's parents' home.

What a slap in the face it was to me. How dare this judge have not an ounce of compassion for me and the other neighbors? I would write the prosecutor often and finally they moved him back to his girlfriend's home, and can you imagine two people living together after being involved in a murder? These are two sick people.

The murder took place outside on common ground. My son was un-armed and it was witnessed that my son only took one step, and this guy shot him with a glock gun. I only hoped and prayed my son did not know what happened as it blew his insides apart.

You know, Mr. Graham, not until you can tell me you have experienced a terrible loss like mine of my son will you ever feel the pain and sickness every day as I do, and that his killer is free. I beg you to please understand why guns do need control of some sort. People just cannot take issues into their own hands and use a gun at will. This is insanity.

Perhaps my story will get you thinking about how we must have to regulate our gun laws. It was years ago that as you say we "have to uphold the Second Amendment as it stands." You know this can be changed. How can you not see how terrible it is when a tragedy such as mine happens, and you show no compassion yourself to what people and guns do.

Regards,

Joan C. Mullins

A LETTER TO JOHN McCAIN

To: Senator John McCain

October 16, 2014

Dear Mr. McCain,

I would not expect you to remember me nor my son. We always followed you around, especially when you came to Hilton Head, Bluffton, and Sun City. My son was so excited to shake your hand while you visited Sun City. He was a proud American and was interested in all events that were going on in our "so at that time" beautiful United States of America.

Sadly, he was murdered in November 2010. At this time I not only contacted and asked you, Tom Davis, Mark Sanford, and our Governor Nick Haley to help me in some way to look at gun control, and also that our Fifth Amendment be re-vamped in some way.

Never heard from you nor our Governor. To my surprise, Mr. Graham answered me with a general letter: "Thank you for contacting us." Then another general letter from him saying he believed in gun control and the up-holding of the Second Amendment.

"Dear Sir," I asked, "have you ever had a child murdered?" He did not respond because he has a staff that takes care of only what has to be told to them to do. So sad. No compassion.

Now for Mr. Davis, I wrote and told him, "Why should I

support you when you are not supporting me? Money is what you want, and I wanted my son back. Reality told me 'no.'"

And another surprise: The office of Davis called me to say "If you want to speak in Columbia, you can do this," but my son's case had not come to trial and I had to say "no" at that time.

My son's case never came to trial, saying "For lack of evidence."

I contacted Davis's office once again, asking if I could go and speak in Columbia. This time I was never contacted again.

But listen to this: A gambling law in South Carolina stopped a community from playing board games. They wanted help, so they asked Mr. Davis to help. He did, and he presented a bill to change things so they could continue with the games.

Here I ask for help as well, and get nothing. I thought, "Why?" My conclusion is that gun control and the Fifth are sensitive issues, and he might be afraid to talk about them for fear of losing his political seat. Where is the courage to be strong enough to face these issues?

Sanford's office had an aide call me, saying "I have been with him for many years.'" "Yes, OK!" I said. I then was asked "What is it you want?"

I replied that I would like to see the Fifth be re-vamped in some way, as it is the criminal that benefits from this law.

This is what I was told: "Your request will be sent to each office: Senators, Congressman and if it is not liked it will be thrown in to the garbage." This is how we are treated? I am an American Mom wanting to tell a terrible horrid story of why my son was murdered. A law made back in the 1500's needs looking into, as it lets a killer go free.

Also I contacted the Attorney General's Office. A reply from them: "Thank you for contacting the South Carolina Attorney General's Office. It has been determined that we can provide you no further information with this case. Our office has reviewed and made our decisions within the constitutional laws of the State of South Carolina." The subject line including the number 8428, referring to my contact number.

What are they talking about? As a victim I am privileged to know anything about this case and my son's death. What information do they have that I do not know about?

My son's murder was senseless, all because a neighbor had his garage door opener that they would not give back to him.

So here it is, election time, and ONLY at this time am I contacted by the Republican Party to give, give what I can. What have they given me? Nothing in response to my request for their support, which I have never had. I must tell you that today I received a phone call from the Republican Party as it is time for these phone calls to start, but not any other time of the year to find out the interest of a Republican voter. They do not care.

So this guy announces, "I am with the Republican Party." I quickly said "I am not interested." And he, very upset, says "What do you mean you are not interested?" I hung up.

The 14th Solicitor was of no help either. I really thought he would be on my side to see an admitted killer go to trial.

The state said that there was not enough evidence, when in fact a verbal police tape is evidence, as is the physical evidence that my son was murdered from a distance of thirteen feet, point blank, when he was unarmed. Once again, my request was ignored. I was even told that the killer did not have a trial, so therefore he is not considered guilty of the crime, even though the killer admitted to the crime. Is this not confusing? Take the fifth, and you are excused from the killing, maybe to kill again?

I asked for this case to be opened again, and guess what? The solicitor just stood there and shook his head "NO." How am I to fight a system when they really do not care that an innocent man was murdered and taken away from his family?

This brings me to the end of this letter, with you asking me to support you, when how can I support any of you? When I needed your help and support, I never received it.

Is it out of your realm that an ordinary human being, I being a mom, that I am asking for help to bring Justice to my son, as this killer is out and about for a murder?

I am asking for your support. Our amendments definitely need re-vamping.

My son's case is an open case, and I hope some day the killer will get what he deserves.

Oh yes, I have written a book about my son's murder. It is called "The Ending." Please look for it, as it will have all the information that I have told you about in my letter to you, and of course how I have been treated by the Justice System.

Respectfully,

Joan C. Mullins

Dear Reader,

Thank you for reading my story. If you can take the time to contact the Beaufort County Solicitor's Office or the South Carolina Attorney General's Office to ask the authorities to re-open Tommy's case for trial, I would be eternally grateful to you, on behalf of my late son. Thank you.

Joan

ABOUT THE AUTHOR

Joan C. Mullins was born in Jersey City, New Jersey. Moving to South Carolina many years later, she began to paint and to write some short children's stories for the entertainment of her own, and with thoughts of her children, grandchildren and great-grandchildren, that they might some day enjoy them as well. For a time, her stories were tucked away in a closet. "Reading them again gave me a chuckle," she says. Since then, her work has been published, and even produced on the stage in the Lowcountry.

Unfortunately, little did Joan C. Mullins know that some day she would be writing a story about the murder of her son, Thomas L. Mullins, Jr.

She can be contacted at: 1artlover123@gmail.com